In the beginning . . . Creativity

Works by Gordon D. Kaufman

Relativism, Knowledge and Faith (1960)
The Context of Decision (1961)
Systematic Theology: A Historicist Perspective (1968)
God the Problem (1972)
An Essay on Theological Method
(1975; third edition, 1995)
Nonresistance and Responsibility, and Other Mennonite
Essays (1979)
The Theological Imagination:
Constructing the Concept of God (1981)
Theology for a Nuclear Age (1985)
In Face of Mystery: A Constructive Theology (1993)
God—Mystery—Diversity:
Christian Theology in a Pluralistic World (1996)

In the beginning . . .
Creativity

Gordon D. Kaufman

Fortress Press
Minneapolis

IN THE BEGINNING ... CREATIVITY

The prologue to this volume was originally published as "God," by Gordon D. Kaufman and Francis Schüssler Fiorenza, in *Critical Terms for Religious Studies*, ed. Mark C. Taylor. Used by permission of University of Chicago Press.

Cover Image: © Photodisc
Cover Design: Kevin van der Leek
Interior design: James Korsmo

Library of Congress Cataloging-in-Publication Data

Kaufman, Gordon D.
  In the beginning ... creativity / Gordon D. Kaufman.
     p. cm.
  Includes bibliographical references.
  ISBN 0-8006-3684-8 (paperback: alk. paper)
  ISBN 0-8006-6093-5 (hardcover: alk. paper)
  1. God. I. Title.
  BT103.K38 2004
  231--dc22   2004008046

The paper used in this publication meets the minimum requirements of American National Standard for Information Sciences—Permanence of Paper for Printed Library Materials, ANSI Z329.48-1984.

Manufactured in the U.S.A.

08   07   06   05   04   1   2   3   4   5   6   7   8   9   10

In memory of
Dorothy

Contents

The maker and father of this universe it is a hard task to find, and having found him it would be impossible to declare him to all mankind. . . . If then, Socrates, in many respects concerning many things—the gods and the generation of the universe—we prove unable to render an account at all points entirely consistent with itself and exact, you must not be surprised. If we can furnish accounts no less likely than any other, we must be content, remembering that I who speak and you my judges are only human, and consequently it is fitting that we should in these matters accept the likely story and look for nothing further.

Plato, *Timaeus*

begin with a paraphrase of the opening verses of the Gospel of John: "In the beginning was creativity, and the creativity was with God, and the creativity was God. All things came into being through the mystery of creativity; apart from creativity nothing would have come into being."

For a good many years I have been speaking and writing of God as *creativity* rather than creator (more recently as *serendipitous creativity*). It has seemed to me impossible—in this age of cosmological and evolutionary thinking, which emphasizes an understanding of our universe as having come into being in and through a Big Bang some 14 or 15 billion years ago—to make sense of the traditional defining idea of God as "creator of the heavens and the earth." By 1975, with my book *An Essay on Theological Method,* I had come to the conclusion that all theological ideas—including the idea of God—could best be understood as products of the human imagination, when employed by men and women seeking to orient themselves in life. This freed me to experiment with a variety of ways of thinking of God, humanity, and the world more congenial to modern/postmodern consciousness about these matters than were (as it seemed to me) the more traditional formulations. But it was not until the publication of my book *In Face of Mystery: A Constructive Theology* (Kaufman 1993a) that I was able to set out in some detail the major problems I had with traditional Christian thinking about these matters, together with my own constructive proposals addressing these problems.

Many have expressed interest in my theological reconstructions, and many have also raised serious questions about my proposals. In a number of articles in recent years I have sought to clarify some of the ambiguities and difficulties in these proposals as well as to develop them further. In the course of these activities I was led to reflect more fully on just what it might mean to think of God not as a personal being who had created the world and everything in it, and who continues to work creatively in and upon that world, but rather as neither more nor less than just this *creativity itself* (however that is to be understood) manifest throughout the vast cosmos as we today think of it.[1] Particularly awe-inspiring to humans, of course, has been the creativity manifest in the emergence of life on planet Earth with, on the one hand, its evolutionary expansion in countless directions and, on the other hand, the painfully slow evolutionary developments that at long last brought us humans—creatures capable of becoming consciously aware of this magnificent panorama of which we ourselves are part— into being, creatures who can and do stand in awe and gratitude before the serendipitous creativity that has brought all this forth and has given us life.

In this book I seek to explore more fully than I have in the past what it means to speak of all this as a manifestation of *creativity*: what we can say about this creativity, how we can think about it, and why it has seemed to me appropriate and illuminating to think of this creativity as God—to think of God as nothing more nor less than precisely this creativity. These are complex and difficult matters, and it is not until the concluding chapter of this book—chapter 3, "In the beginning...Creativity"—that they can be taken up directly. The earlier chapters, including the prologue, are intended to provide a context for, and are thus preparatory to, the exposition in chapter 3. These preparatory chapters were, for the most part, written before chapter 3 was clear in my mind. The ideas to be found in them were themselves also preparatory in that they present some of the steps on my path to this larger picture; they have, however, been reworked and edited for this book. They do not constitute a tight argument culminating in chapter 3 but they do present snapshots, one could say, of scenes along the path to that chapter. In this way they set out a number of contextual matters about which readers of chapter 3 need to be aware in order to understand what is going on there.

The prologue, entitled "The Word 'God,'" sketches the broad historical background and context of this book. Francis Fiorenza and I published this essay (in a slightly different form) in the book *Critical Terms for Religious Studies* (Kaufman and Fiorenza 1998). It sets the stage for chapter 3 (as well as chapters 1 and 2) by recounting briefly the origins of our word "God," and some of the history of its development and employment during the past four thousand years. The meaning of this word is extraordinarily complex (as we today receive it). Fiorenza and I have attempted to make this clear by presenting a quick sketch of the interplay and interconnectedness of three quite different "strands" in its meaning, strands clearly visible in its history throughout the past two thousand years. In its various current uses the word "God" continues to bear all three of these strands of meaning, and we will not understand aright the many quite diverse possibilities for further development in the meanings and uses of this word, if we are not fully aware of this complexity. There simply is no single right or correct meaning—no "essence"—of the word "God." As the prologue shows, it has been open to a great variety of uses and interpretations, and those who wish to think clearly about how it can or "should" be used today—and what we "should" take it to mean today—must be prepared to give reasons for their preferences; no one is in a position to take for granted that they know definitively what the word "God" means and that their use of this word should therefore be assented to by all other English speakers.

These are important points to have clearly in mind while reading the other chapters of this book, because these chapters advocate and argue for a somewhat new and distinctive meaning—for Christian theology—of this word. I have designated this background presentation of the meaning of "God" as a prologue to the argument of the book (rather than its first chapter) because this material basically clears the air of certain misconceptions that might get in the way of understanding what is going on in this book. The argument in this prologue is complex and extended, and for this reason some readers may prefer to move directly into chapter 1, taking up the material in the prologue at some later point in their reading.

Chapter 1, "Today's Evolutionary/Ecological World and the Theological Structure of Christian Faith," is the beginning of the book's argument. This chapter briefly sketches a significant dissonance between traditional Christian understandings of humanity in the world under God and today's evolutionary/ecological thinking. But it falls short of setting out a full presentation of the main reasons for calling into question this Christian thinking (what is designated in this chapter as the *theological structure* of traditional Christian faith). It falls short, in the first place, by not taking into account the great variety of Christian faithing, and by being so very brief in what it does present. And it falls short, in the second place, by moving so quickly and sketchily (in order to introduce my theological proposals) into a presentation of three terms that I have found useful in my constructive work: humans as *biohistorical* beings; the widespread *serendipitous creativity* manifest in the cosmos as conceived today, which provides a promising way of thinking of God today; and the notion of cosmic, evolutionary, and historical *trajectories* or *directional movements* that have emerged spontaneously in the universe at large and on planet Earth in particular, and through which the consequences of the divine creative activity in the world become visible to us humans. It is, of course, impossible to deal properly with these massive issues in the course of a single chapter, though the brief presentation there should give readers some sense of the issues with which this work is concerned. Readers who want a larger and fuller argument on these matters should look to my book *In Face of Mystery* (Kaufman 1993a).

This chapter also focuses on one of the major issues that theologians must today take into account, namely the (partial) responsibility of Christian thinking, attitudes, and practices for the current ecological crisis. After sketching briefly some of the problems that our modern/postmodern ecological ways of thinking raise with respect to some traditional Christian ideas and language, the chapter suggests (with the aid of the three concepts mentioned above) that a different, more ecologically sensitive way of understanding Christian faith and Christian thinking about humanity in the world under God is available to us and should be considered. In this way chapter 1 introduces the reader to the major issue to be addressed in this book, namely, how shall we think about God today?

Chapter 2, then, "On Thinking of God as Serendipitous Creativity," focuses the project of the book further by briefly elaborating my specific proposal that we think of God as the serendipitous creativity manifest throughout the cosmos (rather than as *the Creator* of the world and all that is in it). This chapter (an earlier version published as Kaufman 2001a) was written as a kind of quick introduction, on the one hand, to my proposals about how we should imagine God today, and, on the other hand, as a brief answer to some of the more severe criticisms of these proposals. Like Chapter 1, it does not provide a full argument on the issues taken up (fuller accounts can be found in Kaufman 1993a, 1995, and 1996a), but it does directly present my central proposal about how we should think of God today, and it responds briefly to some of the questions that may arise, especially for readers encountering this proposal for the first time. In this way it introduces some of the central issues that the book is intended to address, thus putting the reader in a position to move on to chapter 3, where an enlarged discussion of what it means to think of God as *creativity*, to think of creativity as *God*, is to be found. I shall not summarize the content of that chapter here.

Despite the extended time that I have reflected on the ideas now presented in chapter 3, I continue to find myself somewhat uncertain about what to make of them. I sent copies of an earlier draft of this chapter to a number of friends whom I thought might be interested in it, asking them to be severe in their criticism, pointing out what they took to be major problems with it but also what positive values there might be in pursuing it further. I got eight responses, some of them enthusiastic about the project, others quite critical of it. These comments were all very valuable, enabling me to improve the text in many ways as well as to avoid a number of serious mistakes, and I am grateful for the time and effort my friends put into their responses. Chapter 3, as it now stands, is a much better piece than I could have made it simply on my own.[2] Though I am still somewhat uncertain about what all this comes to theologically, I have decided that it should be published as a kind of experiment in thought.

The book concludes with an epilogue on the development of my theological thinking. A few years ago I was asked to present an intellectual autobiography at one of the meetings of the Highlands Institute for American Religious and Philosophical Thought. Afterward several persons told me that the statement presented there enabled them to understand better what I was attempting to do theologically than anything else of mine they had heard or read, and they urged that it be published. I continued to work on it, expanding somewhat from what was originally presented, and in due course it was published in the *American Journal of Theology and Philosophy* (Kaufman 2001b). Since this piece sketches the path that led to the conclusions set out in this new book, making some excerpts from it available here to readers should be helpful.

This book is a work in progress. It proposes a way of thinking about God significantly different from most traditional ideas, though it retains and builds upon the central motif in that traditional thinking, that God is the *creativity* that underlies and grounds all that is. I present my formulations here as an option to be considered as we search for ways to bring this symbol at the heart of most Western religious thinking and activity into more intimate and vital relation with today's modern/postmodern understandings of the world, and human existence in the world. Only if we can continue to see God as active in the world as we know it, and thus active in relation to us humans living in this world, will it be possible for us to orient ourselves, and significantly order our lives, in relation to God—that is, to live with a robust faith in God.

The Word "God"

The word "God" is one of the most complex and difficult in the English language, a word rich with many layers and dimensions of meaning. It is full of problems and difficulties—for religious believers as well as unbelievers—and is susceptible to many sorts of interpretation. "God" is a word known and used (in one way or another) by everyone who speaks English: a word used in everyday exclamations of surprise as well as in religious meditation, in cries of despair as well as in worship, in curses as well as in prayers. "God" is the term used more often than any other in the language to name the ultimate in reality and value and meaning for humans, but it has also been employed frequently in thoroughly dehumanizing ways. It is not possible, of course, to explore all the complexity and richness of the meanings and uses of the term "God" within the compass of this prologue. The most that can be presented here is a sketch that suggests some of this intricacy of meaning along with some of the reasons for it.

This historical survey, written with Francis Schüssler Fiorenza, was originally published (in a slightly different version) as Kaufman and Fiorenza 1998.

1

There have been many studies of the idea of God characteristic of this or that historical period, or found in the work of one or another philosopher or theologian. But comprehensive attention to the way in which this symbol itself developed in the course of the past four thousand years or so, its enormous influence on human life and culture throughout that period, and its continuing significance today is scarcely to be found. For some, perhaps, it is simply assumed that "God is dead," and therefore it is no longer necessary to attend carefully to this symbol (even though it obviously still has great power in popular religion); others, who count themselves as "believers" in God, may take one or another more or less traditional understanding so much for granted in their own personal lives that it does not occur to them that this ambiguous, complex, much contested symbol requires careful study in its own right. It might be thought that the guild of professional theologians pursues investigations of the term "God" like those sketched in this prologue, but that is not the case. Most theologians concentrate their attention largely on explication of symbolizations and interpretations found in one particular religious tradition (or a relatively narrow family of religious traditions); the enormous diversity and complexity that this symbol actually carries in our languages and cultures is, in consequence, rarely regarded as of central importance for their work. Despite its continuing importance in human life, serious study of this term is hard to find. This prologue suggests what might be involved in such study.

I. Linguistic and Biblical Backgrounds

The English-language word "God" (spelled with a capital G and with cognates in other Indo-European languages) functions most commonly as a proper name: God is one on whom humans can call in a time of desperate need; God is the creator of the world and of all that is in it, the protector and savior who provides for creaturely wants and who sustains women and men undergoing evils of all sorts; God is one to whom humans should give thanks for the many blessings of life. In the major Western religious traditions, God is the central object of worship and the ultimate court of appeal in all major crises of life.

But who or what is this "God"? According to the *Oxford English Dictionary* (O.E.D.), the proper name "God" (as used in English speech and writing) is linguistically derived from earlier uses (usually indicated by a lowercase *g*) in which the word designates a "superhuman person (regarded as masculine . . .) who is worshipped as having power over nature and the fortunes of mankind; a deity" (O.E.D., 1971, 1:1168). "Deity," in turn, is defined as the "estate or rank of a god; godhood; godship. . . . The divine quality, character, or nature of God" (675). The discussion begins here with "God" as a proper name since "throughout the literary period of English [this has] been the predominant" usage, and what had been "the original heathen sense" of the word came to be "apprehended as a transferred use of this; 'a *god*,' in this view, is a supposed being put in the place of *God*, or an imperfect conception of *God*." In "the specific Christian and monotheistic sense" of this word, which has long been standard in written English, the name "God" has designated the "One object of supreme adoration; the Creator and Ruler of the Universe," and it was often used "in contexts where the One True God is contrasted with the false gods of heathenism" (1168). As these quotations from the O.E.D. suggest, the text of the Bible has been the principal source of the conceptions of God that have dominated spoken and written English, and radical departures from biblical notions (whether in reflective philosophical or theological works, or in esoteric [religious or other] writings)—though often incorporating metaphors, images, and concepts drastically different from any found in the Bible—nevertheless have always (in significant respects) depended for their intelligibility in English-speaking cultures on the force of the basic biblical images and conceptions.

The Bible is a collection of writings produced over a period of at least two millennia and as such includes many different images, concepts, and ways of thinking about what is referred to there as "God." Though the conception of God that dominates biblical texts as they have been appropriated in English-language usage is monotheistic, traces remain of earlier polytheistic and henotheistic uses out of which biblical monotheism gradually emerged. During the early period, when the tribes of Israel lived a nomadic form of life, God was understood as the god of the tribe. A plurality of gods was envisioned, as suggested, for example, by reference to "the God of Abraham and the God of Nahor" (Gen. 51:53). The first commandment also presupposes this view: "I am Yahweh your God . . . you shall have no other gods before me" (Exod. 20:2-3; Deut. 5:6-7); this commandment does not dispute the existence of other gods, but demands exclusive veneration of Yahweh by the Israelite tribes. A god (*El*) of this sort was usually associated with a particular location and its traditions. The development and spread of the *Sinai* traditions led to an understanding of God as "Yahweh," the local god of Mt. Sinai who was honored by Kenites and Midianites. In the later exilic and post-exilic periods, the belief in God as creator became established, as Israel articulated its convictions about Yahweh in confrontation with the cosmogonic notions of new cultural and religious environments. Thus, the claim of Yahweh's exclusiveness eventually developed into Israel's monotheism.

In English-language Bible translations the image/concept "Lord" is used most frequently (much more frequently than "God") to characterize God; in many versions of the biblical text this term is used to translate "Yahweh"—a name that traditional Jews have regarded as too holy to pronounce. This dominant use of "Lord" (a title rather than a name) to refer to God connects directly, of course, with the O.E.D.'s basic characterization of God as the "Creator and Ruler of the Universe." Many other images and concepts, which deepen and expand the notion of God the Lord—nearly all of them male-gendered—are also to be found in the Bible. Some of these are essentially extensions of the notion of lord (king, mighty one, creator, father, shepherd); others, however, bring in strikingly different metaphorical meanings (the first and the last, the most high, the holy one, spirit, love). For the most part, the Bible presents readers with an essentially anthropomorphic image/concept of God: God is sometimes pictured as having arms and legs, eyes and ears, a nose, a mind, a will; God has feelings of anger, kindness, vengeance, mercy; God's actions are purposive and creative, and they manifest righteousness and justice, faithfulness, strength of will, loving kindness, care for God's creatures, a strong commitment to keep promises made in covenants with them. In short, God is presented as an all-powerful, all-knowing moral agent who has brought the world into being and who is continually working in that world—especially with men and women—to carry out the purposes for which it was created.

These largely anthropomorphic images are, however, significantly qualified by a number of profoundly abstract metaphors that give the biblical image/concept of God its sense of utter difference from the human, its sense of overwhelming authority and power—that is, that enable this symbol to refer to *deity* (as contrasted with all finite realities). God is portrayed as saying, for example, "I am the first and I am the last" (Isa. 44:6; cf. 48:12, 41:4; Rev. 1:17, 2:8, 22:13); God is said to be the reality "in [which] we live and move and have our being" (Acts 17:28), a reality present everywhere (apparently at all times), not only in heaven above or "at the farthest limits of the sea" but even "in Sheol" (Ps. 139:8), the last place of the wicked and the dead; God is frequently referred to as the "Most High"; God is presented as having created the heavens and the earth, as being the ultimate source of all that is. None of these expressions and conceptions are *anthropomorphic* or *anthropocentric*, human-like, human-centered (although the activity of *creating* is depicted in anthropomorphic terms in Gen. 1 and 2); all are quite abstract, so much so that, taken simply by themselves, they present no specific content at all. What they express is God's unsurpassability, God's uniqueness. God is *eternal*, a uniqueness of an entirely different order from that of any finite being.

In consequence, what would otherwise appear to be quite straightforward anthropomorphic or anthropocentric locutions frequently become qualified in rhetorically powerful ways: "For as the heavens are higher than the earth [says the Lord], so are my ways higher than your ways and my thoughts than your thoughts" (Isa. 55:9). God's profound incomprehensibility to humans thus becomes an important theme. In the New Testament, for example, Paul writes that God "has mercy on whomever he chooses, and he hardens the heart of whomever he chooses. . . . Who . . . are you, a human being, to argue with God?" (Rom. 9:18, 20; cf. Job 38–42). And Jesus is reported to have reminded his followers that many of God's activities are not what humans would regard as morally discriminating: "your Father in heaven . . . makes his sun rise on the evil and on the good, and sends rain on the righteous and on the unrighteous" (Matt. 5:45). It is often suggested in the Bible that no one ever has direct or immediate contact with or experience of God: in John's Gospel (1:18) and again in 1 John 4:12, it is stated flatly that "No one has ever seen God." The figure of God as portrayed in the Bible (even though in many respects quite anthropomorphically conceived) remains to very deep levels beyond human comprehension or understanding: "How unsearchable are his judgments and how inscrutable his ways!" (Rom. 11:33)

In the Bible itself, thus, the anthropomorphic and anthropocentric qualities so important to those who pray to and worship God are not what in fact establish God's *deity*; it is, rather, those locutions which drastically qualify human-like characteristics that distinctively identify God as *God*. And it is their presence as essential components of the biblical image/concept of God that makes it possible for worshipers to employ this symbol in directing their feelings and thoughts and activities toward what they regard as ultimate reality, power, and meaning. Nonetheless, the anthropomorphism of the biblical God and the overall anthropocentrism of the biblical story of God's activities remain throughout, and in some Christian texts these are strongly accentuated: "God so loved the [human] world," we are told, "that he gave his only Son, so that everyone who believes in him may not perish but may have eternal life" (John 3:16).

The biblical God has been regarded, in many quite different sociocultural contexts, as the ultimate reality and power, and thus the ultimate authority figure for humans. There have always been, however, sharp disagreements about how God is to be conceived and understood, due at least in part to the great diversity of images and concepts that (as we have seen) are used to characterize God in the Bible, and the tensions of many sorts to which this diversity inevitably gives rise. Heretics were burned at the stake or drowned, and terrible wars were fought, over such issues; so-called unbelievers were persecuted, tortured, killed; and campaigns of enslavement and genocide were undertaken—all in the name of the holy and righteous God of the Bible. The God claimed to be the creator, sustainer, and savior of humans from all manner of evils has, on many occasions, "authorized" utterly bloodthirsty crimes of humans against each other. This God has also, of course, frequently provided the inspiration for resistance to injustice and tyranny as well as movements toward more responsible and humane patterns of human life.

II. Three Strands of Meaning in the Term "God"

We have thus far considered only one of the strands that constitute the meaning of the word "God" as it is employed in English-speaking societies—the *biblical* strand, which contributed the basic structure and many of the images that comprise this meaning-complex, providing it with much of its sociocultural, personal, and religious-spiritual energy, creativity, power, and authority. The Christian movement, however (the principal bearer of this symbol during the formative period of Western culture), grew into a major religious and sociocultural force largely within Hellenistic culture, and was heavily shaped in many ways—including in its use and understanding of the image/concept "God"—by Greek and Roman (in addition to Jewish) traditions and practices. Thus the term "God"—already very complex, as we have noted—was to become much more elaborate and complicated in its strands of meaning and in its uses than has so far been suggested.

It has sometimes been supposed that the great diversity of thinking and feeling and attitudes respecting God could be sorted out and assessed by distinguishing sharply between what philosopher Blaise Pascal (1623–1662) called "the God of Abraham, Isaac, and Jacob" (that is, the God of biblical traditions) from "the God of the philosophers and scholars" (*Memorial* in Pascal [c. 1670] 1995). But the intermixing of Greek and Hebraic traditions in Western religious history has become so intricate and mutually interconnected that such simplistic attempts to disentangle the various dimensions of meaning that this word now bears inevitably fail. Consider, for example, the uses to which the word "trinity" (a term central in Christian understanding of God) has been put. "Trinity" is not a biblical word at all but acquired its meaning originally in highly technical, theologico-political discussions of a range of terms drawn from Greek (and Latin) philosophical reflection (*ousia*, *hypostasis*, substance, essence, persons, modes, etc.). Nevertheless, in such phrases as "Blessed Trinity" it is widely used in the liturgies and prayers of many ordinary worshipers. Similarly, in the historic creeds (often given a central place in worship) technical philosophical language about "two natures" in "one person," and the like, is to be found. Not only have philosophical ideas been integrated in this way into central devotional activities and practices; in the Bible itself (as noted above) profoundly abstract notions, deeply qualifying the prevailing anthropomorphic imagery, also perform indispensable functions. Claims that Greek conceptions of God are philosophical—and hence conceive of God as immutable—while the biblical understanding is anthropomorphic and more suitable in worship are inadequate on other counts as well: they overlook the extent to which the Bible, especially the Christian writings, is itself permeated with Hellenistic cultural and philosophical views, and they fail to take note of the anthropomorphic, polytheistic images in Greek mythology.

Though some might still wish to separate out these various historical strands in meaning, which the symbol "God" has come to carry in Western languages and cultures, this is not likely to illuminate matters much since the word "God" itself, as employed today, inevitably carries traces of all this complex weight of meaning. A more adequate approach recognizes that both anthropomorphic and philosophical ideas and images of God are to be found in every historical period in Western history—Judaic, Hellenistic, and Roman antiquity as well as the medieval, Reformation, and modern periods. It is precisely this richness and intricate complexity of meaning that gives this word its continuing significance in human life and praxis.

Instead, therefore, of attempting to identify the exact historical roots of various strands of meaning borne by the word "God," three of the complex patterns of, or tensions in, meaning that have emerged in the course of Western history will be discussed here, each of which contributes significantly to the meaning(s) that "God" bears today. The first complex is concerned with the distinction already mentioned, between (on the one hand) popular images and models for conceiving God and (on the other) more reflective and philosophical language. Some popular images seem to dominate certain periods but may not be employed much in others, and these differences are themselves often correlated with the social and political practices and beliefs characteristic of each period. Philosophical categories, attitudes, and questions also change drastically over time. Consider, for example, the enormous impact modern science and philosophy have had on reflective, as well as popular, thinking about God.

The second complex of meaning concerns the relation of language about God to the understanding of human subjectivity and creativity. Whereas in antiquity it was often assumed that the reality of God is interior to, and thus directly present within, the soul (e.g., Plotinus, Augustine), in modernity this way of thinking has become both more complex and more problematic. Human subjectivity (from Descartes to Rahner) is thought of as permeated by an awareness of infinity (not "God" as such), and a critical awareness of the creative and constructive role that human language itself plays in precisely this consciousness increasingly emerges.

These developments prepare the way for consideration of our third complex of meaning: *negative theology*, the awareness and articulation of the inadequacy of *all* human language and ideas about God. This is a theme, going back to the first centuries of the Common Era, that has reappeared in every period and found new forms of articulation in modernity/postmodernity. There have been, however, significant changes along the way, with emphasis shifting from a focus on the attributes of the *object* of theological inquiry—God—to much more concentrated attention on the intrinsic limitations of all human knowledge.

These three complexes of meaning in concert contribute significantly to the tensions, complexity, and force of the term "God" today, as well as to an intrinsic indeterminateness in its meaning that makes agreement on its proper specification and articulation difficult to reach.

III. The Conflict between Philosophical and Popular Images of God

The early Christian theologians appropriated Greek philosophical thinking in a very selective manner to elaborate their understanding of God. They criticized the Skeptics and Epicureans but took over elements of Stoic speech and thought about divine providence. Above all, they appropriated Platonic and neo-Platonic ideas about the divine that were regarded as useful in criticizing popular Greek and Roman mythological language. The emphasis on unity in neo-Platonic philosophy was employed in criticizing Greco-Roman polytheism, for God conceived as "one" and "unchangeable" stood in sharp contrast with popular language about the actions of various deities on behalf of particular cities, locales, or persons. The early Christians were called "atheists" because, in denying the existence of the gods of the polis, they undermined popular beliefs in Greco-Roman deities. However, this embrace of Platonic philosophy by Christians also presented some large problems. For example, the incarnation of God in Jesus meant that God *changed* through entering the world of time, history, and matter. The attempt to understand this led to the gradual development of the concept of the Trinity (often regarded as the most distinctive mark of Christian thinking about

God). But Christian belief in the Trinity had then, in turn, to be reconciled with the Hellenistic idea of God's oneness.

The affirmation of the oneness of God goes back to Plato's adoption of the Pythagorean method of seeking explanation in mathematical terms. The ultimate principle of all reality, order, and goodness is to be found in the origin of all numbers, the *One*. God, the originative source of all being, was not dependent upon any other being, and was thus the sole ultimate being, without beginning, without change, without parts, existing from all eternity. This Greek understanding was linked with the biblical God of Exodus, "He Who Is" (cf. Exod. 3:14), in both Jewish (Philo of Alexandria [20 BCE–54 CE]) and Christian theology. The philosophical emphasis on oneness also had a popular political connotation since it was associated with the Roman monarchy: the one divine ruler of the universe and the one emperor on earth were seen in intimate connection. In the East, the debate about the Trinity, therefore, was not only an issue about Christian orthodoxy but involved a critique of political monotheism as well.

The distinction between everyday popular usage of the term "God" and philosophical language using other terms became important in the medieval period. Anselm of Canterbury (1033–1109) consistently replaced the popular term "God" with philosophical terminology more appropriate to his argumentation. He used such terms as *summa essentia, summus spiritus,* and *ipsum bonum* to refer to the divine. This distinction between a philosophical and a popular use of language is also evident in Thomas Aquinas (1225–1274). The individual "proofs" or "ways" to God's existence resulted in a philosophical principle, such as "unmoved mover" or "first cause." Aquinas concluded that these refer to "what everyone calls God."

At the same time popular thinking about God in terms drawn from the feudal social system was current even among sophisticated theologians. Anselm's classic theory of satisfaction is based upon a feudal conception of justice with its emphasis on honor and debt: the human debt to God is infinite because human sin went against the (infinite) honor of God and therefore can be satisfied only by an incarnate God. And Thomas Aquinas explained divine providence in terms of the popular imagery of a king setting goals, even though he thought of the divine causality in neo-Platonic and Aristotelian conceptions. Jean de Gerson (1363–1429) not only argued that one had to keep to the traditional term "God" but also affirmed the importance of the sovereignty of God who ruled the world with the control of an absolute ruler. Nicholas of Cusa (1401–1464), however, underscored the inadequacy of all language respecting God, even the term "God." He argued that it is necessary to have the greatest number of descriptions, of which he preferred the terms *maximum pariter et minimum* and *unum absolutum* (Nicholas of Cusa [1440] 1954, 1:4).

Medieval theology thus sought a synthesis between philosophical ways of speaking/thinking and the God of revelation. But the rise of medieval nominalism, represented especially by William of Ockham (1285–1347), led to a breakdown of this synthesis. For Ockham, not only does God's free will determine what is necessary for salvation but God's free choice can be discerned only through divine revelation. This voluntarism provided a philosophical context for the Protestant Reformation, which emphasized the radical corruption of human nature through sin and the conviction that humans know God only through revelation. For Martin Luther (1483–1546) the causal ontological grounding of theological and philosophical speaking and thinking of God recedes in favor of an emphasis on God's free activity. Although John Calvin (1509–1564) acknowledges a sense of the divinity within humans and the witness of creation to God's existence, all such natural knowledge is considered confused, hindered by sin, and thus incapable of leading to true knowledge of God. The latter, to be found only in the scriptures, was available to all believers and not simply to academic theologians or spiritual mystics. The Reformers thus conceived God less in categories such as absolute simplicity or principle of unity of being and more as the Divine Monarch with a sovereign will (in keeping with the political context of the increasing power of national monarchies). Here the inscrutable will and freedom of the sovereign God, rather than the simplicity and unity of the uncreated principle of all Being, comes into the forefront of language and conceptions about God.

The religious wars of the sixteenth and seventeenth centuries led to the acceptance of religious tolerance as a necessity for political life. They also led to a critique of the dogmatic claims in the religious confessions (most of which were formulated largely in "popular" terms). Two movements in this early modern period, the Enlightenment and pietism, are important for our concerns here. Though pietism is often seen as a reaction to the Enlightenment, these two developments nevertheless had similar features in their thinking of God: they both emphasized religious subjectivity (either through an analysis of consciousness or through emphasis on the believer's religious experience), and they underscored the practical relevance of faith. The use of more personal language about God, strongly emphasized in the Reformation period (especially in left-wing groups), steadily increased, with deism using the image of God as watchmaker and pietism employing personalistic familial metaphors. Despite these commonalities, however, sharp differences between Enlightenment and pietistic rhetoric and thinking led to a decisive split between popular imagery of God and the philosophical critique of such language. Georg W. F. Hegel's (1770–1831) philosophy of religion attempted to overcome this, but a dualism between philosophical reflection and popular religious language became dominant in the modern period, and a great proliferation of ways of speaking and thinking of God appeared.

Although Darwinism sounded the death-knell for a natural theology of design, attempts to conceive God in philosophical categories based upon a scientific understanding of the world have continued. William James's writings on pragmatism and religion, for example, present a scientific democratic conception of religion and divinity. *The Varieties of Religious Experience* ([1902] 1985) points to the specific and irreducible nature of religious experience and its enlargement of human consciousness. In *A Pluralistic Universe* ([1909] 1977) James advances the notion of the divine as finite (as had John Stuart Mill [1806–1873]) within a pluralistic universe: "'God,' in the religious life of ordinary men, is the name not of the whole of things, heaven forbid, but only of the ideal tendency in things" (124). James regards the idea of an "'omniscient' and 'omnipotent' God . . . as a disease of the philosophy-shop" (James 1920, 269).[1] In his view of the universe as pluralistic, "God" signifies a reality that is finite in both knowledge and power but calls forth an active human response; humans can cooperate with God in effecting changes in the world.

Quantum theory brought an end to the mechanistic worldview of Newtonian physics and thus encouraged the development of notions of God as in process. In contrast to the emphasis of traditional theism on the divine simplicity that entails immutability and infinity, the process theisms of Alfred North Whitehead (1861–1947) and Charles Hartshorne (1897–2000) distinguish between the abstract essence of God (as absolute, eternal, unchangeable) and God's concrete actuality, which is temporal, relative, changing, and dependent on decisions made by finite actualities. Hartshorne, moreover, claims his language about God is more biblical and personal than that evoking the God of classical theism. In Whitehead's understanding, God offers to each "actual occasion" that possibility which would be best but does not control or determine the finite occasion's self-actualizing; God works by persuasion and is not in total control of the events of the world. The existence of evil in the world is thereby compatible with the divine beneficence toward the world.

In these and other similar developments there is a continual crisscrossing of popular and reflective images and conceptions nurturing and fertilizing each other, giving birth to widely different ways of speaking and thinking of God. So the meaning(s) of the word "God" have expanded in many directions, producing rich new possibilities for its employment but also much disagreement about how it is to be used, and many have begun to wonder whether it can any longer be usefully employed. Nevertheless, the power of this symbol remains great in popular Western culture, particularly in North America, and theologians and philosophers of quite diverse commitments continue to struggle with its meaning for human life in today's world.

IV. Subjectivity and the Word "God"

In the classical tradition, in keeping with the prevailing anthropomorphism and androcentrism of earlier conceptions and images of God, the spirituality of the soul was regarded as the avenue to knowledge of God as Spirit, and this influenced decisively the way in which the term "God" was employed (especially in "reflective" uses). This focus continues into modernity, although now the emphasis is placed more on the dynamism of the human intellect, which in its striving to unify experience is taken to be the source of our ideas of God. This modern development opened the door for historical studies and the sociology of knowledge to call attention—in connection with their exploration of the social and linguistic character of all human knowing—to certain social and political features of language about God as well as to the practical consequences in human life of the diverse images employed in this language. These all have had their effects on the meaning and uses of the term "God" today.

The idea of God as Spirit, pure Being without material parts, led classical Christian authors to approach the understanding of God largely through reflection on the self. In his *On Free Choice of the Will*, Saint Augustine (354–430), for example, holds that human intelligence is the highest and best of human attributes. This intelligence is dependent upon a reality that is higher than itself, the spiritual, eternal, and unchanging God ([388-95] 1993, 2.37–15.39). Since the soul is the image of God, Augustine asserts in *The Trinity* that the mystery of the trinity can be understood (to some extent) through analogy with the human soul: just as self-knowledge, self-memory, and loving self-affirmation are interrelated, so too are Father, Son, and Holy Spirit ([400-16] 1963). The soul's knowledge of itself leads to knowledge of God and to a true idea of being.

This approach to God through subjectivity, however, undergoes a decisive shift in the transition to modernity. René Descartes (1596–1650), seeking to establish knowledge upon a secure foundation, called into question everything that could be doubted until he reached an indubitable proposition: "I think, therefore I exist." Then, through establishing a criterion of truth (what is clearly and distinctly perceived) and the existence of God (as an infinitely perfect being who cannot deceive), he made the idea of the infinite the condition of the knowledge of all finite objects (since these objects are delineated as limited only in relation to this idea). Descartes's approach left the modern West with a twofold legacy: (1) a *foundationalism* that equates knowledge with secure foundations and clear and distinct ideas, and (2) an emphasis on subjectivity that anchors the knowledge of God but leaves the world of nature "godless."

This decisive shift in the understanding of subjectivity's importance is connected with other cultural developments. As the Newtonian and mechanical worldview was increasingly established as the only legitimate scientific position, a move from theism to deism takes place. The terms "deism" and "theism" were originally synonymous, but "deism" came to refer to the view that the divine lacks an immediate ongoing personal relation to the world. God was often pictured as a watchmaker: once the watch was made, it ran according to its own mechanism. Having established natural laws, God does not intervene in ways contrary to them, that is, miraculously. David Hume's (1711–1776) critique of the metaphysical view of causality and his demolition of the argument from miracles advanced a naturalistic view of the world, and in the nineteenth century Charles Darwin's theory of evolution further undercut natural theologies, with evolution providing an alternative explanation to divine teleology. These developments in the natural sciences eliminated God entirely from the order and design of the material world. Christian theology had long distinguished the traces of God in the sensible and material world from the image of God in the soul, but in modernity this distinction became a rupture, with the locus of

God for humans restricted to subjectivity—pious subjectivity without objectivity.

F. D. E. Schleiermacher (1768–1834) sought a post-Enlightenment understanding along this line by locating religion in human feeling, not understood as an emotion but rather as an immediate self-consciousness or a mode of experiencing oneself in relation to the totality of the universe. This religious dimension of experience became, then, the locus for language about the divine. In his *On Religion: Speeches to Its Cultured Despisers* ([1799] 1958), he uses such terms as "universum," "infinite," "world-soul," and "All" to replace the idea of an all-powerful person. Such terms focus attention more on the unity and infinity of the universe than on a personal God (thereby picking up on widely influential ideas earlier developed by Baruch Spinoza [1632–1677]). G. W. F. Hegel, however, argued that both the Enlightenment critique of metaphysics and the location of language about God in religious feeling robbed the idea of God of its proper meaning: in Christianity the divine idea is the unity of the divine and human nature, not as a static structure but as a trinitarian *movement* of "self-othering" and self-reconciliation. Thus, what is originally present in religious belief as a "representation" and objectification becomes elevated into a (philosophical) *concept* that transcends the representational in its validity. God as spirit is triune, a conception of the divine that enabled Hegel to overcome dichotomized understandings of the relation between God and the world, between the infinite and the finite.

In the left-wing Hegelian movement, however, the social construction of language about the divine came to the fore, exemplified in the critique of religion found in Bruno Bauer (1809–1882), Karl Marx (1818–1883), and Ludwig Feuerbach (1804–1872). In his *Essence of Christianity* ([1841] 1957), Feuerbach argues that when humans attribute qualities to God, they are actually calling attention to those human qualities they consider most valuable. To affirm that God is love, for example, is to affirm that love is divine. However, by projecting these qualities onto an object other than the human species, one alienates the human species from itself as well as from the world of nature. Feuerbach thus brings out not only the constructive character of language about God but also the alienating effects of such language. Friedrich Nietzsche (1844–1900) further radicalizes the critique of religious belief in his proclamation that "God is dead" (a phrase already used by Hegel) and his critique of Christian theism as a popularized Platonism. His analysis of the "will to power" shows how theistic valuations and beliefs introduce dominative powers that alienate humans from nature and life.

In the period following World War I, under the impact of the cultural crisis it provoked, a strong "neoorthodox" protest against these sorts of developments occurred, beginning with Karl Barth's (1886–1968) emphasis, in his *Epistle to the Romans* ([1918] 1933), on the "infinite qualitative distinction" (a Kierkegaardian phrase) between God and everything human. Given this understanding, Barth claimed that God could be known only through God's own activity, that is, divine revelation. Though Barth's intent was to overcome in this way the human-centeredness of theologies rooted in human subjectivity and religious experience, he accomplished this by employing a concept of God (held to be drawn from the Bible) as a fully self-conscious, volitional, self-revealing being, a supreme *Subject*—ironically building on central human metaphors. Thus, though neoorthodoxy criticized modern theology for its emphasis on subjectivity and its "humanization" of language about God, it too mirrored this emphasis by employing the categories of modern (androcentrically conceived) subjectivity in its understanding of God. Whereas the medieval tradition interpreted God as the "to be of being," Barth, though seeking to demolish the modern theological emphasis on the human subject, nevertheless conceived God essentially in these modern terms.

During the same period that Barth was working out his theology of revelation in Europe, Shailer Mathews in the United States was proposing, in *The Faith of Modernism* (1924) and *The Growth of the Idea of God* (1931) that the social scientific study of religion investigate the relation between social mind-sets and religious beliefs.

Mathews surveyed the idea of God through seven social mind-sets: Semitic, Hellenistic, imperial, feudal, nationalist, bourgeois, and scientific-democratic. Whereas the Semitic mind-set views Christ as a messianic king within the scenario of the world drama between God and Satan, the Hellenistic mind-set recasts the messianic expectation into the concept of the *logos*, God's creative "Word." The imperial mind-set casts God as a universal emperor, the feudal mind-set sees redemption in terms of the honor due God as a feudal lord, and the nationalist mind-set envisions God as a political monarch with absolute authority. Mathews ends his survey with the scientific-democratic social mind-set. The task of theology is to understand God in a way that coheres with this current dominant way of thinking; in 1915 Mathews emphasized the democratic pattern, whereas in 1930 he emphasized the scientific pattern. His proposals made explicit the modern awareness of the interrelation between human consciousness and religious language, between social mind-sets and religious beliefs. His work not only shows the extent to which conceptions of God are always built up out of metaphors at hand in the culture but also underscores the necessity for theological methodological reflection and construction to take into account the current social and political institutions and conditions, as theologians and others attempt to ascertain (that is, construct) the meaning of the term "God" in a specific historical context.

This methodological awareness of the social and linguistic conditioning of language about God came to the fore in the twentieth century in discussions of the nature of religious language. Some seek to explore what is distinctive about religious language or about "God-talk" by examining specific types of language, such as "limit" expressions; others ask whether religious language involves speech-acts that entail a specific existential commitment of the speaker as well as propositional affirmations. According to another approach religious language cannot be defined in essentialistic terms. It is a mistake, thus, to speak and think of it in any of these essentialist ways: religious language is always part of a life-praxis and can be understood only within that specific context (Ludwig Wittgenstein). Yet another approach emphasizes the openness and creativity of all metaphors: Paul Ricoeur has proposed that biblical language about God be explored in terms of the creativity of its literary forms and its metaphors, while Sallie McFague's *Models of God* (1987) and Gordon Kaufman's *In Face of Mystery: A Constructive Theology* (1993a) present programs of God-talk in basically metaphorical terms.

The images and metaphors used to express the divine are taken from several areas: the family and personal relations, various occupations, political life, the world of nature, modern scientific thinking. Images from the family often convey the intimacy of a personal relation (God as father, mother, friend, helper). Images drawn from occupations provide examples of particular activities that may be regarded as presenting important ways of viewing the divine (shepherd or caretaker, potter, builder, warrior, or commander). Other images are drawn from political life (king, lord, master), from nature (spirit [wind], force, power, ground), and from science (evolution, ecology, field of force). The use and implications of these images may be quite diverse. On the one hand, to imagine God as king encourages attitudes of submission and obedience (to God) in ways that the images of friend or comforter do not. On the other hand, images of Christ as king or lord have often served to draw contrasts with totalitarian regimes, as in the anti-Nazi position of the German Confessing Church; the allegiance to the divine ruler serves, in this case, not as a source of submission but rather as a resource for resistance.

H. Richard Niebuhr has emphasized that more fundamental than the question of God's existence is the question of the kind of God we have. In *Radical Monotheism and Western Culture* (1960) he points to God as a transcendence that undercuts all human idols, including church, the scriptures, and Christ. Niebuhr explicates Christian belief in the trinity by showing how it protects against various sorts of one-sidedness in life. If God is identified only as father, then one tends to see the created order in terms of the will of God (creator of that order) and its fulfillment; however, if God is identified mainly as

Christ the savior, then salvation and redemption, in contrast to the present created order, are emphasized; if God is viewed exclusively as spirit, the ecstatic elements in religious life become highlighted. Here the trinity, with its images of God as father, son, and Holy Spirit, has implications not only for the conception of God but also for the understanding of human life.

Contemporary feminist theology has challenged the largely male-gendered traditional image of God as father because of its reinforcement of patriarchal institutions and values. In *Beyond God the Father* (1973) Mary Daly not only criticizes the system of patriarchy entailed in this image but also attacks the static and dualistic metaphysics implicit in it. In seeking to overcome the inadequacies of exclusively identifying the symbol "God" with such symbols as father and lord, feminist theologians have taken different directions. Sallie McFague has sought to offer alternative images such as mother, friend, and lover (cf. the classic trinitarian imagery of father, son, and holy spirit). Elisabeth Schüssler Fiorenza, a New Testament scholar, highlights the role of the feminine Sophia-God within the Wisdom traditions of the Bible and the identification of Jesus in the early strands of the New Testament traditions as the messenger of this Sophia-God, and then later with Sophia herself. In a different direction, Carol Christ (see especially 1997) and others argue for the necessity of a post-Christian approach to God-language. They retrieve the image of the Goddess from non-Christian, especially pre-Christian, traditions and argue for its significance. Rosemary Radford Ruether explicates the notion of "Gaia" in relation to the understanding of God (a name that she frequently writes as God/ess).

All of these more recent approaches ask what kind of God we have, thus exploring further the meaning and use of God-language. The increasing proliferation of metaphors and images, of course, and the growing critical awareness that each has significant limitations raise the question of the adequacy of all God-talk—an issue at the center of the tradition of negative theology, to which we now turn.

V. Negative Theology and the Word "God"

As reflective modes of thinking about God develop, awareness of the limitations of human knowledge of God becomes increasingly acute; already in the Bible there are poignant references to the hiddenness and inscrutability of God, as observed earlier (section I). It is not surprising, then, that early Christian writers, alongside their positive theological speaking and thinking, developed a negative theology as well. The Cappadocians, especially Gregory of Nyssa (335–394), underscored the inaccessibility of God to human knowing; the spirituality and infinity of God makes God inaccessible to human knowledge. Pseudo-Dionysius (sixth century) goes further: God's incomprehensibility does not flow from the limitations of the human mind but is a quality of God. John of Damascus in *Exposition of the Orthodox Faith* ([c. 743] 1899) and Pseudo-Dionysius in *On the Divine Names, and Mystical Theology* ([sixth century] 1951) affirm that one can only posit negative statements about God. Moses Maimonides (1135–1204), an influential medieval Jewish thinker, argues similarly: the oneness of God means not only that there is not a plurality of gods, but also that God as unique is beyond all human creatures; propositions about God are, therefore, negations ([1190] 1963, 1, 58). For both Pseudo-Dionysius and Maimonides we can affirm what God is not, not what God is; similar conclusions are reached by Islamic philosophers such as Avicenna (980–1037) and al-Ghazzali (1058–1111).

Medieval theology developed an explicit theory about the uses of analogical language in speaking of God, and this doctrine of analogy is often contrasted with negative theology, in that analogy entails not only negative but also positive affirmations about God. Correctly understood, however, the theory of analogy does not so much affirm the adequacy of positive affirmations as the imperfection of all language about God; it should be seen, thus, not as rejecting but as continuing the tradition of negative theology. Thomas Aquinas, in *Summa Theologiae* ([1271] 1964, vol. I, question 13) distinguishes between an analogy of attribution and an analogy of proportionality. An analogy of attribution is based upon similarity between cause and effect: eating vegetables, for example, can be called healthy because it produces health. An analogy of proportionality, however, points only to a proportion between two elements in realities that are to be sharply contrasted with each other. Thus, God's understanding and wisdom are proportionate to God's being, and human understanding and wisdom are proportionate to the being of humans. This type of analogy underscores *dissimilarity* rather than similarity, when human language and images are applied to God. God is infinite and human beings are finite and limited: no proportionality exists between God and humans. In applying propositions to God, one is indeed making an affirmation but only imperfectly, and what is affirmed has to be affirmed in a way that negates and transcends the finite analogue. As Aquinas notes in the introduction to question 3 of the *Summa Theologiae:* "Now we cannot know how God is, but only how God is not; we must therefore consider the ways in which God does not exist, rather than the ways in which he does exist." The theory of analogy is, thus, close to a negative theology.

A more radical negative theology is found in the writings of the mystics. Meister Eckhart (1260–1328), for example, held that being and knowing are identical, and what has most being is most known. But from this he concludes, "Because God's being is transcendent, he is beyond all knowledge" ([c. 1300] 1941, 142). Nicholas of Cusa takes negative theology in a speculative direction, going beyond medieval thinking with his notion of "learned ignorance." This was not simply a Socratic not knowing but rather the assertion that one knows *because* one does not know. Arguing that nothing can be greater than the "Absolute Maximum" or less than the "Absolute Minimum," God is beyond all opposition, for in God these opposites coincide (*coincidentia oppositorum*).

In modernity, a distinctive sort of negative theology emerges. It is not so much based on the spiritual nature of God or the infinity of God's being in contrast to human finiteness as on the limits of human reason. Immanuel Kant (1724–1784) sought to provide a firm foundation for rationality by examining the proper use of human reason within its limits. He shows that the cosmological, teleological, and ontological proofs of God's existence all presuppose an ability that the human mind does not have: to go beyond experience and give content to the idea of an absolutely necessary being. Kant's critique of natural theology is not simply that one cannot theoretically demonstrate the existence of such a being; it is the more basic claim that the very notion "existence of God" ensnares speculative philosophy in the dialectical illusion of assuming that God is the sort of object that can be characterized as "existing." The concept of God for Kant, thus, becomes a regulative idea or transcendental ideal. "What this primordial ground of the unity of the world may be in itself, we should not profess to have thereby decided, but only how we should use it, or rather its idea, in relation to the systematic employment of reason in respect of the things of the world" ([1781] 1929, B727). Kant thus develops a negative theology based on the limitations of human knowledge. At the same time, however, his understanding of the function of the transcendental, and of God as a postulate of practical reason and morality, open the way for pragmatic and self-critical reflection on our use of language, images, and metaphors about God.

Johann G. Fichte's (1762–1814) critique of traditional theism goes further than Kant's. Fichte argues that qualifications or determinants such as substance, consciousness, and personhood are all finite and therefore cannot be applied to God. Personhood is finite, for example, since a personal subject is determined by things outside of itself and becomes conscious of itself only in relation to other finite objects. To transfer the anthropomorphic category of personhood (an individual self-conscious self) to God goes against the infinitude of the divine. Fichte's conclusion led to misunderstanding and to the charge of atheism.

Influenced by Kant's critique of theistic metaphysics and Fichte's critique of personhood, Friedrich Schleiermacher sought to redefine the understanding of religion and the divine in his *On Religion: Speeches to Its Cultural Despisers* ([1799] 1958). In his *Christian Faith* ([1822] 1928) and *Dialektik* ([1811] 1976), Schleiermacher explicates the believer's immediate self-consciousness as an experiencing of the self as "utterly dependent." As he goes on to note, the "whence" of this utter dependence is what religious persons and believers name God, but what a non-religious interpretation calls nature. In his discussion of the adequacy of religious statements about this "whence," Schleiermacher is conscious of the Kantian critique: religious affirmations are more properly propositions about the human condition than metaphysical descriptions about God or the world; the attributes of God, thus, do not refer to something specific in God but rather express our relation to God. Schleiermacher does go beyond this, however, insofar as he views the diverse divine attributes as expressing the one divine causality. ("Causality," of course, is simply the correlate of the sense of a "whence.")

In postmodern philosophers and theologians a more radical critique is advanced. Here it is not simply the epistemological issue that is raised, but also the *onto-theological* question. (Behind this postmodern challenge stands the influence of Martin Heidegger [1889–1976] with his view that the distinguishing characteristic of modern philosophy is its tendency to think of Being in terms of subjectivity and its search for an indubitable certitude [René Descartes].) The problem becomes, How does one think of God, or otherwise use the word "God," without reducing God to a being like other beings or an object like other objects? The concern with overcoming these objectifying tendencies so characteristic of the onto-theological tradition is evident in such postmodern thinkers as Marion, Lévinas, and Derrida.

Jean-Luc Marion criticizes the metaphysical conception of God as idolatry. In *God without Being* (1991), he argues that to think of God as the all-comprehensive concept, and as a free willing ground of everything, is idolatrous, for it fails to eliminate empirical threads from the super-sensible notion of God. Emmanuel Lévinas (1906–1995) also criticizes the Western philosophical tradition for its conception of God as a being with certain ontological qualities. For him even Western mysticism sees God as, however mysterious, nevertheless comprehensible by some elect few; this is still to conceive God anthropomorphically and fails to comprehend the otherness of God. In *Totality and Infinity* (1969) Lévinas uses the word "Infinity" rather than "God" to express this otherness. For him the Holocaust reveals the failure of theodicy and the God of ontology, and he proposes that God is known through the ethical relation of our responsibility for others. He finds "traces" of the Good, of the transcendent Other in our responsibility for the other. Jacques Derrida criticizes attempts to appeal to a negative theology, and to seek to distinguish God from being, in his argument that such attempts are still onto-theologies. They continue to use the conceptuality of Platonic and neo-Platonic philosophy even in arguing that God is not being or is beyond being. Though negative theologies seek to go beyond the alternatives of theism and atheism, they are tied to an onto-theology to the extent that they seem to retain a being beyond Being, some hyperessentiality that is beyond all negation and positive predication.

Such critiques radicalize negative theology. They suggest that even in its negations all negative theology is tied to an ontology that presupposes the being of the divine. We seem here, with respect to God, to end up with utter speechlessness. But we should not forget that it has been only through *speaking*—through uttering this enormously complex word "God" and speaking about God, and through speaking in critique of all such speaking—that we may be led to this conclusion.

VI. The Symbol "God" and the Study of Religion

Our sketch of these three meaning-complexes connected with Western employment of and reflection on the term "God" shows how complicated, difficult, but rich this word has been and still is. As an ultimate point of reference for all that is (and, indeed, is *not*), the term is intended to gather up, comprehend, and hold together all reality

and experience, all possibilities and imaginings in a meaningful interconnection that can orient human life—an intention surely tran-
scending all human capabilities of knowing, conceiving, or imagining.
It is hardly surprising, therefore, that the "death" of God has frequently
been proclaimed in modern times. And yet speaking the word "God,"
worshiping God, thinking about God, all continue. The long history
of negative theology, and alongside it and coexisting with it the regular renewal of reflective positive theologies as well as much popular
imagery and language about God, testifies to the continuing importance of this term. The full meaning of these conflicted ways of speaking to and about God, evident throughout the history of God-talk, is
still far from clear.

Much of this prologue has been devoted to sketching the complexity that the word "God" has come to have in the course of
Western history; it is the central, most powerful symbol to which
human life in the West has been ordered and oriented. In modern
times, thus, although it has become highly contested (not only
among intellectuals in the universities, but in wide sectors of
Western culture at large), this symbol is still very much alive. Other
terms, such as the "holy," the "sacred," "divinity," the "supernatural," the
"mystical," and so on, have been proposed as articulating what is at
the heart of religion. None of these common nouns, however,
expresses either the comprehensiveness or the specificity of meaning
to which the proper name "God" adverts, with its positing of an ultimate point of reference in terms of which all realities must be understood, and its claim, therefore, that all aspects of human life (not only
religious and moral practices and experiences) should be oriented in
terms of this reference point. This ultimate point of reference (God)
relativizes all present human practices, ideologies, and institutions,
calling them all into question critically—while demanding their
transformation in more humanizing and humane directions. It is not
evident that the meanings and uses of this rich and complex symbol
can be properly grasped through subsuming it under one or more
such general concepts as those mentioned above; rather, it must be

carefully examined in its own right, not reduced to something else quite different.

What kind of study is required to bring this enormous complexity of meaning into proper focus? How can religion studies contribute most effectively to the exploration, understanding, and interpretation of this symbol? We suggest here the usefulness of three different approaches. Each of these can help bring into view important dimensions of the symbol "God" and the way it functions, and all of them taken together, and interconnected with each other, should produce a richer and more profound understanding than anything now available. Only an interdisciplinary "field-encompassing field" such as religion studies has the capability of pursuing a project of this scope and depth. In view of the power and significance this symbol has had in the past and continues to have, this sort of concentrated effort would seem to be appropriate.

(1) **Historical, sociological, and other analytical studies of the symbol "God."** One type of study that needs to be pursued much further is of the sort this essay begins to sketch: a much fuller and more careful analysis of the origins of this symbol, the various streams of tradition that have contributed to its development, and the many diverse cultural and linguistic contexts in which it has played a significant role in ordering and orienting human life. In addition to such historical studies, we need much fuller knowledge than we presently have of the way in which the word "God" continues to function in a range of cultural contexts today. There are, for example, those popular religious movements for which "God" is a central rallying cry and focus for devotion as well as for political action, movements including (but not limited to) some that are often designated as "fundamentalist" or "evangelical." Many persons, however, who are not directly associated with such movements, also count themselves "faithful believers" in God. What does this word mean to such believers? How do they understand the God in whom they place their faith? Why do they regard faith in God as important? How do they relate themselves to their neighbors who do not profess such faith? Does their faith lead

them to church involvement or regular biblical study? And so on. Non-reductive sociological, psychological, linguistic, and other studies of what "God" actually means to diverse groups of modern/postmodern people, and what importance (or lack of importance) this word has for them, are much needed.

(2) **Comparative studies of "God" and "the gods."** Much academic study of religion is directed today by interest in history of religions and comparative religions. Early in the last century comparative studies of the symbol "God" (and "the gods") were beginning to get under way, but for many decades these have been in abeyance, perhaps in part because of the Western bias evident in many of those earlier studies. Properly done, such studies would involve not only comparative examination of the diversity of linguistic traditions involved—their grammatical and syntactical practices and their uses of various sorts of metaphor; exploration of the differing ways in which major ordering symbols (like "God") function in these diverse traditions; and so on—but also the ritualistic, moral, and social contexts with which these linguistic practices are connected. Comparative studies of this sort should help to call into question—and to challenge—Western theistic and atheistic biases that may still operate in the studies proposed under (1) above, by introducing totally different conceptual frameworks for ordering, orienting, and reflecting on human existence and activities. One thinks, for instance, of the illumination the Buddhist notion of *sunyata* (emptiness) could bring to the problems posed by Western substantialist thinking about God, a way of thinking that has given rise (as we have seen) to the long critical tradition of negative theology.

These two sorts of studies taken together should bring fuller understanding of the diverse ways in which (at least some) religious symbol-systems have actually functioned in a range of sociocultural contexts, thus providing a basis for developing more adequate theories of religious symbolization than are now available. Such theories, in turn, should facilitate more disciplined examination of the alleged uniqueness of the symbol "God" as well as more adequate assessment of its actual strengths and weaknesses. Without better understanding of these issues the questions regarding this symbol posed by, for example, today's growing consciousness of the significance of religious pluralism, can scarcely be addressed intelligently.

(3) **Constructive work.** With these various sorts of studies all in mind, a further question needs address: can (or should) the symbol "God" be deliberately *reconstructed* today in ways that will enable it to order and orient the lives of modern/postmodern people more effectively? Attempts to construct imaginatively new, more viable, meaningful, and self-critical ways to conceive, understand, and employ the symbol "God" in today's world comprise the central task of *constructive* theology (see Kaufman 1993a, 1995). Theological work has always been a constructive—and/or reconstructive (Fiorenza 1984)—activity, engaged in imaginatively as women and men have had to come to terms with new contingencies, new issues, new problems. Today many different sorts of issues call into question various features of traditional (Western) understandings of God: issues posed by religious pluralism; by scientific cosmologies; by the increasing economic, political, cultural, and religious tensions between the powerful "First World," or industrialized, societies and other less powerful sectors of our global village; by the moral, intellectual, religious, philosophical, and other forms of criticism (including, most recently, feminist criticism) to which the symbol "God" has been subjected in the last two or three centuries, both in the West and in parts of the world that the West colonized; and so on. These can be taken up in more deliberate and self-conscious fashion now than has ever before been feasible. Radical, far-reaching deconstructive work, together with highly imaginative fresh construction and reconstruction, is beginning to appear in the studies of theologians of many different stripes. In due course all of this should have significant effects on the way the word "God" is understood and used in the future, though doubtless much "popular" religion will continue to resist these developments.

The significance of constructive work with the symbol "God" can be considered from another vantage point. What bearing (if any) do the various sorts of technical studies described under (1) and (2) have for the actual *faith in God* of thoughtful women and men in today's world—reflective members of churches and synagogues and mosques, as well as interested persons who do not have communal or institutional religious commitments? Should those involved in the academic study of religion be concerned with "practical" questions of this sort? Do religionists have responsibilities to the wider society and culture that sustains them to assist in the address of major problems faced in that society and culture? Or is the study of religion a "purely academic" exercise? The natural and social sciences, as well as some of the humanities, are drawn upon in diverse ways for the knowledge and understanding necessary to address major problems that today's societies confront. Religion studies might also have much to offer if they focused attention more directly on sociocultural problems in which religion and religious symbols are deeply implicated and if they sought to address more directly some of these matters. We think that scholars in the study of religion do have responsibilities of this kind. They ought, therefore, to be developing proposals about how the enormous confusions concerning God, and faith in or loyalty to God, might be addressed in modern/postmodern societies.

Are some ways of thinking of God today more responsible than others? Is it important (or feasible) for modern societies to address sensitive theological questions of this sort (in view of the enormous sociopolitical power that the symbol "God" still commands)? In what ways do some of the individuals and groups that use the word "God" quite freely in fact seriously *mis*use it? And what sociocultural consequences does this have? Is it appropriate to speak of "proper" and "improper" uses of this word? What should loyalty to God today involve? These questions call attention to important issues that should be much more freely discussed and debated in the public square than they commonly are, and such discussions should in no way be foreclosed by governmental or ecclesiastical authorities. In American society—with its well-known "wall" separating church (or religion) and the state, though the name of God is widely invoked in contexts (often government-sponsored) of "civil religion"—surely more public attention to what is involved when the word "God" is employed is called for. More direct address of this deep *theological* root of public life in this society might help soften some of the hard-edged discourse becoming increasingly prominent in our public life. It is, of course, to the sorts of constructive studies mentioned in the last three paragraphs that the several chapters in this book—especially chapter 3—are devoted.

The study of religion is one of the few disciplines that is in a position to begin addressing the problems that arise in connection with the centrality of the symbol "God" in our historical past and its continuing force in public life. But taking up this social/cultural/political task has rarely been considered by scholars in this field to be their responsibility, and hence studies in religion have not been organized in ways that focus directly on these matters. Religion scholars should at least ask themselves whether they may not have some distinctive responsibilities, *qua* religion scholars, with respect to these central problems in our society about which they are almost alone in having expertise. As Robert Bellah said years ago, "in the last analysis [humans are] responsible for the choice of [their] symbolism" (1970, 42). Religion scholars have a special obligation to help modern societies exercise that choice responsibly. In this book special attention is devoted to the question whether the symbol "God" is today functioning as effectively as it might and should—in our modern/postmodern world—and a specific proposal to address this problem is presented.

Today's Evolutionary/Ecological World and the Theological Structure of Christian Faith

ll too often it is thought that theology (thinking about God) and faith in God are two more or less independent features of human existence—that men and women can be faithful believers without caring a fig about theological questions and that much theological work is of a conceptual sort that can be carried out insightfully whether one is a believer or not. There is some truth in each of these claims. But it would be a mistake to assume that theological work and faith are irrelevant to each other, for all Christian faith is given its basic structure by the two polar symbols that it takes for granted—human being and God.[1] Believers may regard their faith in God as that which is of central importance to their lives, even though they may never have stopped to inquire about the particular characteristics of the *idea* of God that they hold, simply taking it for granted that it is indeed *God* in whom their faith is placed. But the way in which we envision God (and Christ) determines in important respects characteristics and qualities of our faith and of our living out the requirements laid upon us by that faith. And the situation is similar, of course, with our (largely taken for granted) understanding of our humanness.

All of us have taken over, for the most part, the meanings of the terms "God" and "human" that we initially learned early in life as we acquired the English language, and these have become complexified for us and developed in various ways by the religious and other traditions into which we have been socialized, as well as by our own personal experience. These two terms (like all words) get their meanings in part through their close connections with a range of other words, such as "faith," "life," "devotion," "creation," "commandments," "forgiveness," "love," "worship," "idol," "Bible," "omnipotent," "morality," and so on. The many complex interconnections of this symbolic polarity—*God* and *humanity*—with other words enable it to provide a deep structure that informs and orders our self-consciousness, our experience, and many of our activities, a structure taken for granted in much of our living and thinking.

But what if this deep structure—in the form that we have acquired it—no longer fits well with the world in which we live and thus, instead of orienting us with respect to that world, misleads and disorients us? What if the traditional meaning of the two symbols, *God* and *human*, which give this polarity its basic content and significance—however important, appropriate, and effective they have been in ordering the lives of many generations before our time—are no longer as pertinent as they were in the past to major problems that humans must today address? What if they seem to increasingly require reinterpretation, reformulation, reconstruction, or even outright rejection? What if there seems to be no place for what has been called "God" and "God's activity" in the world as we today think of it? The questions about how we think of God—whether that understanding can work for us any longer—and how we think of ourselves, how we understand our humanness, have been under heavy fire for the last two or three hundred years. Clearly no consensus about the meanings of these important symbols prevails any longer, either within the churches and synagogues and mosques or in the wider culture.

In face of this situation, what should thoughtful persons do? Some appear to be ready to ignore this symbolic polarity upon which

Western civilization has drawn through much of its history: "God is dead!" they have been telling us for a century and more. Many others, though not using such dramatic language, find themselves pursuing their practical day-to-day lives with little concern about either God or humanity as they search for, and seek to live out of, significantly different symbolic forms (whether secular or religious). In my view, though God may be dead or largely irrelevant for many in our world, this symbol remains much more powerful and meaningful than any other, not only in the West but in many other places around the globe as well. Both because of its continuing power, and also because that power is so often put to exceedingly destructive abuses—consider the many bitter and brutal ethnic and other wars still pursued today in the name of God—those of us who have significant commitments to this symbol have good reasons to carefully explore its seeming lack of fit today. And that may put us into a position to reconstruct the two interrelated symbols of God and humanity in ways that will enable them to orient and guide our lives more appropriately and effectively. In the prologue of this book we have taken note of the enormous diversity, complexity, and richness of meaning of the symbol "God," which can be drawn upon in such reconstruction.

In this chapter we shall further examine this symbol—in its interconnection with the image/concept of the human—using the contemporary ecological crisis as a lens to help us discern what is at stake today in the employment of this symbolic polarity. First, I shall outline briefly some of the features of our received religious thinking about God and humans that tend to make the employment of traditional understandings of the symbol "God" problematic in today's ecologically-sensitive world. Second, I shall propose some significantly different models for thinking about God, humanity, and the relationship between the two. These models, I shall argue, can enable us to more effectively connect these two major symbols to significant features of our modern conception of the world and to widely accepted assumptions about how human existence in this world must be understood today. This will, third, put us into a position for a fresh take on what faith in God might mean in today's world, and we will be able to see how such faith can focus our attention on and illuminate some of the frightening problems with which we humans must now come to terms, as well as help motivate us to address those problems with courage. In short, in this chapter I shall sketch briefly a different way of imagining God than our religious traditions have taught us; in chapters 2 and 3 this sketch will be developed in considerable detail. It will, I hope, enable us to see better how important faith in God still can be, as we seek to come to terms with some of today's major problems.

I

A largely unspoken assumption throughout much Christian history has been that faith and theology are concerned basically with what we have come to call the *existential* issues of life—despair, anxiety, guilt, death, meaninglessness, sin, and the like. Beliefs about God's love, mercy, forgiveness, justification by faith, and so on addressed these issues of meaning and finitude and sinfulness, thus enabling life to go on. This focus and imagery, I suggest, encourages an understanding of both the Christian God and Christian faith in fundamentally human-centered terms—as concerned, that is, largely with certain deep personal problems.

This *anthropocentric* focus of Christian thinking appears at many points. It is clearly expressed, for example, in the idea that humans (unlike all other creatures) were made in the very "image of God" as the climax of creation. It is also visible in the traditional notion of God itself, constructed as it is on the model of a human being, a human agent: God has been thought of as in many respects human-like. Thinking of humans as made in the image of God—and that God in turn is like a human in significant ways—was not just employing some lovely ideas. They were ideas that provided theological grounds for a fundamentally *dualistic* understanding of the human—a two-sided, body-and-soul kind of thinking—that has characterized Christianity through most of its history. According to this view, though we share bodiliness and animality with other parts of the creation, that which distinguishes us most clearly from the rest—our spirituality, our souls—images God's own spiritual being. That which is most important about us, thus, is that we are souls, spirits, and we are uniquely related to those heavenly beings whom we will join when, with death, we depart this physical world. As was discussed in the prologue, God has largely been thought of as a kind of cosmic spirit who loves humankind and for this reason entered directly into human history to bring salvation. Because of this intimate interconnectedness of God and the human in the traditional Christian story, it was believed that we could have confidence that there will always be a Christian answer to every really important issue that might arise for women and men anywhere and everywhere. With God—the very creator of the heavens and the earth, the ultimate power in the universe—so closely interconnected with humans (especially those who are Christians!), how could it be otherwise?

Today, however, we find ourselves in a period beset by serious issues significantly different from the existential problems of our personhood. With the advent of the atomic age a half-century ago, a great many things began to change. It became evident that we humans had attained the power to destroy the very conditions that make our lives (and much other life as well) possible, and the notion that God would save us from ourselves as we pursued this self-destructive project has become increasingly implausible. Though the vividness of the nuclear challenge has now receded somewhat, the problem it brought to our attention has grown more pressing with our discovery that we humans, especially in modern times, have been destroying the ecological conditions apart from which much of life cannot exist (whether there is a nuclear holocaust or not). Humanity, as we are beginning to understand, is deeply situated within the evolutionary/ecological life processes on planet Earth, and it is becoming increasingly difficult to imagine God as one who might (or even can) directly transform and make right what we are so rapidly destroying. So it is not really evident that God (as Christians have traditionally understood God) provides a solution to what is a major problem for men and women today: the ecological crisis.

This is a different kind of issue than Christians (or any other humans) have ever faced, and continuing to worship and serve a God thought of as the omnipotent savior from all the evils of life may even impair our ability to see clearly its depths and significance. Today the most important religious issue is not how we can find a way to live with or overcome despair or meaninglessness or guilt or sinfulness, or human suffering generally—however significant these problems may be. Now it has to do with the much more basic matter of the objective conditions that make all life—including human life—possible: we are destroying them, and it is we who must find a way to reverse the ecologically destructive momentums we have brought into being.

This is not a specifically Christian problem (though in certain respects Christianity bears special responsibility for it, as we are beginning to see here). It is a problem in which all humans are implicated, and we are all called to do our part in its solution. So the central religious issue confronting humankind today is of a different sort than ever before. And we may no longer claim that Christians have a corner on the solution to it, nor do Buddhists, or Jews, or the adherents of any other religion. What is now required is a reordering of the whole of human life around the globe in an ecologically responsible manner—something heretofore never contemplated by any of our great religious (or secular) traditions. All of humankind must learn to work together on this issue, or it will not be taken care of. Theology now becomes essentially a constructive task, and the symbol-systems of our various religious and secular traditions, in terms of which we do our thinking and acting, our living and our worshiping, have to be reconsidered in light of these problems that so urgently demand our attention.

It is not difficult to understand why the focus of human religions—including traditional Christian faith—has been basically human-centered. However diverse human religious faiths may be in our many different cultures and religions, they were each created as our forebears sought ways (over many generations) to come to terms with the various issues with which life faced them. It should not surprise us, therefore, that the basic focus of these traditional religious orientations has been on what would facilitate survival of the community—of the tribe, of the people—who worked together and faced the problems of life together, who sensed they belonged together. The God of Israel, for example—Yahweh (Jehovah)—was originally a savior-God who (it was believed) brought the people of Israel out of Egypt in dramatic displays of power and led them into military victory as they invaded Canaan, the land that Yahweh had promised them. Yahweh was the one on whom they could always call when life became unbearable, horrible, unintelligible, as can be seen clearly in the many cries to the Lord in the Psalms, in Job, in Jeremiah, and elsewhere throughout the Hebrew Scriptures. The Christian story, when it appeared, built on this heritage, maintaining that God was so deeply involved in the human project on Earth as to come down to Earth in the person of the man Jesus to rescue humankind from all the evils of life, bringing an eternal life of perfect human fulfillment. The whole story here—the very idea of God in these traditions—is thoroughly human-centered. God was imagined primarily in terms of metaphors drawn from human life—God is thought of as a lord, a king, a father, a mighty warrior, and so on; humans regarded themselves as made, in their distinctiveness from the rest of creation, in the very "image and likeness" of this God, and God's activities were centrally concerned with human life and its deepest problems.

This kind of deep structure in the *God-human symbolic complex* that underlies and forms the faith-consciousness and faith-sensibility in the three religions stemming from ancient Israel (Judaism, Christianity, Islam)—and is most powerfully accentuated in Christian faith, because of the centrality there of God's incarnation in Christ—inevitably gives rise to a fundamental tension (indeed a conceptual and logical incompatibility). It is the tension between, on the one hand, this received understanding of God and of the intimate relation of humanity to God and, on the other hand, our growing awareness that human existence is actually constituted by, and could not exist apart from, the complex ecological ordering of life that has evolved on Earth over many millennia.[2]

The symbol "God"—not nature, it is important to note—functioned during most of Western history as what we could call the ultimate point of reference in terms of which all human life, indeed all reality, was to be understood. God was believed to be the creator of the heavens and the earth (as Genesis 1 puts it), the creator of "all things visible and invisible" (as declared in some of the creeds), the lord of the world. It was, therefore, in terms of God's purposes and God's acts that human existence and life—indeed, all of reality—were to be understood. As we have noted, God was seen as essentially an agent, an actor, one who is doing things; and human existence was to be oriented most fundamentally on this transworldly God, not on anything in the world (that is, in the order of nature). For humans to orient themselves and their lives on anything other than God and God's acts was deemed idolatry—a turning away from the very source and ground of humanity's being and life and a direct violation of God's will for humankind. However, as the context and ground of human life has become thought of increasingly in evolutionary and ecological terms (as in modernity and postmodernity), nature has become a direct rival of God for human attention and devotion.

For many centuries, nature and God were not in any sort of significant tension with each other, since what we today speak of as "nature" was thought of as God's creation—the world—in every respect a product of God's creative activity and at all points completely at God's sovereign disposal. The concept of an *autonomous nature*, as we think of it today, had no real place in the biblical story at all. That story was focused, rather (as we have noted), on Yahweh and Israel, God and humanity: the divine-human relation was clearly the axis of this story around which all else revolved. And in the end when God will create "new heavens and a new earth" (Isa. 65:17; Rev. 21:1), this will be primarily for the sake of the "new Jerusalem"—a new human order where all suffering, pain, and misery will be overcome (Isa. 65:18-24; Rev. 21:2-4). The rest of creation, though always recognized and sometimes acknowledged and carefully studied, simply was not of central theological interest or importance and (with the exception of the angels) never became the subject of any technical theological vocabulary or doctrines.

If, however, we think of the reality with which we have to do largely in the ecological terms increasingly used today—in terms of the interconnected and interdependent powers and processes of nature, instead of such more traditional religious terms as God our "heavenly Father" whose children we are, or the "Lord" of the universe whose loyal subjects we seek to be—we are led to sharply different understandings of who or what we humans are and how we ought to live. To the extent that we today take our experience of *natural* powers and processes as central in our understanding of reality—rather than the distinctly *human* activities and experiences of choosing, setting purposes, willing, thinking, creating, speaking, making covenants, and the like, which provided principal models for constructing the traditional symbol "God"—we are thinking of the world in which we live, and our human place within it, in terms quite different from those presented by our Western religious traditions.

To sum up my remarks to this point: the traditional Christian understanding of humanity in relation to God, with its powerful human-like God-idea and its belief that humans are created in the image of this God, tends to obscure and dilute (in Christian faith and theology) ecological ways of thinking about our human place in the world. We need to ask ourselves: Is it necessary today to develop an understanding of God and humanity that overcomes these difficulties? Can the symbols "God," "world," and "humanity," and their relationships to each other, be constructed in a way that enables them to highlight our ecological embeddedness in the natural order rather than obscure it, thus helping to orient us, in our living and our actions, in ways directly appropriate to our place in that order? Should Christian faith today come to understand itself in a new symbolic pattern of this sort, as it seeks to shape its living and acting in today's world? I want now to present a brief reconstruction of these three interconnected symbols that is coherent with our modern/postmodern evolutionary conceptions of the appearance and development of life on Earth and of human existence within the ecology of life.

II

Three concepts, taken together, will help us think of God, humanity, and their relationship to each other in a different way than that found in more traditional Christian thinking. First, I want to spell out briefly what I call a *biohistorical* understanding of human life (to replace the more traditional body/soul dualism, the "image of God" understanding). This way of conceiving the human emphasizes our deep embeddedness in the web of life on planet Earth while simultaneously attending to the significance of our radical distinctiveness as a form of life. Second, I want to call attention to what can be designated as the *serendipitous creativity* manifest throughout our evolutionary universe—that is, the coming into being through time of new realities. I use the concept of *creativity* here—rather than the traditional idea of "God the creator"—because it presents creation of novel realities as ongoing processes or events and does not call forth an image of a kind of cosmic person standing outside the world, manipulating it from without. In my view, if we wish to continue using the word "God," we would do well to understand it as basically referring to this ongoing creativity manifest in the cosmos. Third, since the traditional idea of God's purposive activity in the world— a powerful movement working in and through all cosmic and historical processes—is almost impossible to reconcile with modern and postmodern thinking about evolution and history, I propose to replace it with a more modest conception of what I call *trajectories* or *directional movements* that emerge spontaneously in the course of evolutionary and historical developments.

This more open (even random) notion—of serendipitous creativity manifesting itself in evolutionary and historical trajectories of various sorts—fits in with but significantly amplifies today's thinking about cosmic, biological, and historico-cultural processes. It is a notion that can be used to describe and interpret the enormous expansion and complexification of the physical universe from the Big Bang onward, as well as the evolution of life here on Earth and the gradual emergence of human historical existence. This whole vast cosmic process, I suggest, displays (in varying degrees) serendipitous creativity: the coming into being through time of new modes of reality. It is a process that has frequently produced much more than would have been expected or seemed possible, given previously prevailing circumstances, even moving eventually along one of its lines into the creation of human beings with their distinctive history and historicity.

Let us turn, then, to the notion of humans as biohistorical beings. (I take for granted here the basic evolutionary account of the origins of human life.) Let us look briefly at certain features of the later stages of the process through which humankind (as most twenty-first-century university-educated people understand it) actually emerged—that is, was created. Although the modern consensus that humankind emerged out of less complex forms of life in the course of evolutionary developments over many millennia—and that we could not exist apart from this living ecological web that continues to nourish and sustain us—is certainly important, it is too vague and general to provide adequate understanding of the sorts of beings that we humans actually are today. For example, though the natural order is, no doubt, the wider context within which human history has appeared, an exclusively biological conception of human being says nothing about the importance of the uniquely historical features of human existence. It has been, however, especially through their historical, sociocultural development over many thousands of years— not their biological evolution alone—that humans have acquired some of their most distinctive and significant characteristics.

This historical development over many millennia—the gradual emergence of human culture, of human activities and projects—has been as indispensable to the creation of what humans are today as were the biological evolutionary advances that preceded our appearance on planet Earth. Indeed, our human biological nature itself has been shaped and informed in important respects by certain historico-cultural developments. Brain scientist Terrence Deacon has recently argued, for example, that it was the emergence of symbolic behaviors—such as language, a central feature in the historical unfolding of human cultural life—that brought about the very evolution of our unusually large brains (Deacon 1997). And this human history, with its eventual development of highly complex cultures, its diverse modes of social organization, and its exceedingly flexible and complex languages and behaviors, turns out to be the only context (as far as we know) within which beings with self-consciousness, with great imaginative powers and creativity, with freedom and responsible agency, have appeared. All the way down to the deepest layers of our distinctively human existence, thus, we are not simply biological beings, animals; we are biohistorical beings—beings shaped by both biological evolution and historical developments. [3]

These biohistorical processes have transformed our relationship to the nature within which we emerged. As one rather obvious example of this point, consider the impact of the historical growth—over thousands of generations—of human awareness of and knowledge about the natural world around us and about human constitutions and possibilities. Though taking strikingly different forms in the various cultures of humankind, these developments—in some form—are present in all. And in all cultures they have provided women and men with significant powers over their environment and themselves. In the cultures of modernity human knowledge has become increasingly comprehensive, detailed, and technologized, providing us with considerable control over the physical and biological (as well as sociocultural and psychological) conditions of our existence. So humans today, and the further course of human history, are no longer completely at the disposal of the natural order and natural powers in the way we were as recently as ten thousand years ago. Thus, it has been in the course of human history that we humans have gained—especially in and through our various symbolisms and knowledges, skills and technologies—a kind of transcendence over nature unequaled (so far as we know) by any other form of life. Consequently, for good or ill, humans have utterly transformed the face of the Earth, are beginning to push on into outer space, and are becoming capable of altering the actual genetic makeup of future human generations. It is *qua* our development into beings shaped in many respects by historico-cultural processes like these—that is, processes in part humanly created, not simply natural biological processes—that we humans have gained these increasing measures of control over the natural order, as well as over the onward movement of history. In significant respects, thus, our *historicity*—our being shaped decisively by an evolution and history that have given us power to shape future history (and even future evolution) in significant ways—is the most distinctive mark of our humanness.

However, despite the great powers that our knowledges and technologies have given us, we are aware today that our transcendence of the natural orders within which we have emerged is far from adequate to assure our ongoing human existence; indeed, the ecological crisis of our time has brought to our attention the fact that precisely through the exercise of our growing power on planet Earth we are destroying the very conditions that make life possible. Paradoxically, thus, our understanding of ourselves and of the world in which we live, and our growing power over many of the circumstances on planet Earth that have seemed to us undesirable, may in the end lead to our self-destruction. There is, after all, another much greater, more comprehensive creativity than ours going its own way in the universe, and it relativizes, and often overturns, our creative activities, projects, and goals.

This brings us to the other two concepts mentioned above. I suggested that we think of the universe not as a kind of permanent structure, but rather as constituted by (a) ongoing cosmic serendipitous creativity that (b) manifests itself through trajectories of various sorts working themselves out in longer and shorter stretches of time. There are, of course, many cosmic trajectories moving in quite different directions, and here on planet Earth there have been many quite diverse evolutionary trajectories on which the billions of species of life have been produced. Human existence—its purposiveness, its greatly varied complexes of social/moral/cultural/religious values and meanings, its virtually unlimited imaginative powers and glorious creativity, its horrible failures and gross evils, its historicity—has come into being on the trajectory that eventuated in the spread and development of human life over all the earth, the trajectory that issued in the creation of us beings with historicity, this serendipitous manifestation of the creativity in the cosmos that has given us men and women existence. With the emergence of historical modes of being—that is, humans—explicitly purposive (or teleological) patterns appeared in the universe, as human intentions, consciousness, and actions began to become effective. Thus, a cosmic trajectory, which had its origins in what seems to have been mere physical movement or vibration, has (in the instance of human existence) gradually developed increasing directionality, ultimately creating a context within which deliberate purposive action could emerge and flourish. With the help of our three concepts, we are beginning to gain some orientation in the universe as we think of it today.

We do not know what direction this evolutionary/historical trajectory will move in the future: perhaps toward the opening of ever new possibilities for human beings, as we increasingly take responsibility for our lives and our future; perhaps going beyond humanity and historicity altogether, however difficult it is to imagine how that should be understood; perhaps coming to an end in the total destruction of human existence. The creativity in the universe goes its own way, and that way is not always in accord with our human wishes and desires. Like the God of our ancient traditions, however, this creativity is both *humanizing*—it has brought our human reality, with all its values and meanings, into being—and *relativizing*, calling into question and ultimately limiting us and our projects.[4]

Construing the universe in this way, as constituted by cosmic serendipitous creativity that manifests itself in trajectories of various sorts, is important because it helps us see that our proper place in the world, our home in the universe, is the evolutionary-ecological trajectory on which we have emerged. Let us note four points in this connection. First, this approach provides us with a frame within which we can characterize quite accurately, and can unify into an overall vision, what seems actually to have happened, so far as we know, in the course of cosmic evolution and history. The ancient cosmological dualisms—heaven and earth, God and the world, supernature and nature—that have shaped Christian thinking from early on and have become so problematic in our own time, are completely gone in this picture.

Second, this approach gives a significant, but not dominant, place and meaning to the distinctive biohistorical character of human life within the cosmic process and, as a result, the traditional anthropological dualisms—body and soul (or spirit), mind and matter, those beings bearing the "image of God" and those that do not—also fall away in this picture. Moreover, this means, happily, that the basis on which the distinction of male from female has been elevated into a rigid gender dualism is also undercut here. It is important for us to note that the ecological niche that is our home can be properly defined and described only by carefully specifying not only the physical and biological features required for human life to go on, but the significance of certain historical features as well. For example, only in sociocultural contexts in which some measure of justice, freedom, order, and mutual respect sufficiently prevail, and in which distribution of the goods of life (food, shelter, health, education, economic opportunity, and so on) is sufficiently equitable, can children in each new generation be expected to have a reasonable chance of maturing into responsible and productive women and men—women and men, that is to say, who can take the sort of responsibility for their society and for planet Earth that is now required of human beings worldwide.

Third, awareness of these sorts of distinctive biohistorical features of ourselves and our ecological niche makes possible patterns of thinking that can assist communities (and individuals) to better understand and more fully assess both the adequacy of the varied bio-historical contexts in which we humans live today, as well as the import of the diverse sociocultural developments through which the various segments of humanity are moving, in this way enabling us to take up more responsible roles within these contexts and developments. Thus, *normative thinking* directly appropriate to our varied human situations on planet Earth is facilitated by this biohistorical understanding, and the all-too-human-centered moralities and religions, politics and economics, of our various traditions can be more effectively called into question and significantly transformed—another serendipitous manifestation of both the humanizing and the relativizing dimensions of the creativity in the world.

Fourth, because this approach highlights the linkage of cosmic creativity with humanness and the humane values important to us as well as with our ecological niche, it can support hope (but not certainty) for the future of our human world. It is a hope about the overall direction of future human history—hope for truly creative movements toward ecologically and morally responsible, pluralistic, human existence. A hope of this sort, grounded on the mystery of creativity in the world—a creativity that, on our trajectory, evidences itself in part through our own creative powers—can help motivate men and women to devote their lives to bringing about this more humane and ecologically rightly ordered world to which we aspire. If God is understood as the creativity manifest throughout the cosmos—instead of as a kind of cosmic person—and we humans are understood as deeply embedded in, and basically sustained by, this creative activity in and through the web of life on planet Earth, we will be strongly encouraged to develop attitudes and to participate in activities that fit properly into this web of living creativity, all members of which are neighbors that we should love and respect. Thus, we will be led to live in response to, and in so doing will contribute to, the ongoing creative development of our trajectory—God's activity among us humans—within this web. (This interweaving of the divine creativity with ours will be elaborated significantly in chapter 3.)

III

This vision of reality—this frame of orientation—is not, of course, in any way forced upon us: it can be appropriated only by means of our own personal and collective decisions, our own acts of faith in face of the ultimate mystery of life and the world. We humans are being drawn beyond our present condition and order of life by creative impulses in our biohistorical trajectory suggesting decisions and movements now required of us. If we respond in appropriately creative ways to the historical and ecological forces now impinging upon us on all sides, there is a possibility—though no certainty—that niches for humankind, better fitted to the wider ecological and historical orders on Earth than our present niches, may be brought into being. However, if we fail to so respond, it seems likely that humans may not survive much longer. Are we willing to commit ourselves to live and act in accord with the imperatives laid upon us by the biohistorical situations in which we find ourselves, in the hope that our actions will be supported and enhanced by cosmic serendipitously creative events? In my view it is this kind of hope, and faith, and commitment to which the trajectory that has brought us into being now calls us.

Thinking of God as the serendipitous creativity manifest in the world, as I am suggesting here, will evoke a significantly different faith and hope and piety than that associated with traditional interpretations of the Christian symbol-system. However, certain central Christian emphases are deepened. First and most important, understanding the ultimate mystery of things, God, in terms of this metaphor facilitates (more effectively than the traditional creator/lord/father imagery did) maintaining a decisive qualitative distinction between God and us creatures. The creativity manifest in the world now becomes the only appropriate focus for devotion and worship, that which alone can provide proper overall orientation for our lives. All other realities being creatures—being finite, transitory, and corruptible—become dangerous idols when worshiped and made central to human orientation, and they can bring disaster into human affairs. This distinction between God (creativity) and the created order—perhaps the most important contribution of monotheistic religious traditions to human self-understanding—continues to be emphasized in the symbolic picture I am sketching here. Second, in keeping with this first point, conceiving humans as biohistorical beings who have emerged on one of the countless creative trajectories moving through the cosmos—instead of as creatures distinguished from all others as the very image of God, the climax of all creation—makes it clear that we humans are indissolubly a part of the created order. In this picture the too-easy human-centeredness, and Christian-centeredness, of traditional Christian thinking is thoroughly undercut.

The understanding of God proposed here can be developed into a fully-orbed Christian interpretation of human faith and life, if we think of the creativity that is God in significant connection with the poignancy and power of the story and character of Jesus—regarded (by Christians) as what Colossians 1 called the "image of the invisible God."[5] To many today the christic imagery of the New Testament, with its overriding emphasis on self-sacrificial love for others and on communal reconciliation and upbuilding, is regarded as a trap that is destructive of important human possibilities. Others find the christic imagery and stories beautiful and romantic but virtually useless for orientation in the cold "real world" in which we find ourselves, where quite different values and standards are in play. These christic images and meanings remain compelling, however, for they reveal something of great importance to our alienated human life. Notions and stories of reconciliation, love, and peace, of self-giving, voluntary poverty, concern for our enemies, vicarious suffering, point to our deep interconnectedness with each other. Thus they show the direction in which communities and individuals must move if our human world is ever to become more truly humane.

A decent human world will not be created as long as our activities are directed largely by our own self-aggrandizement, whatever the cost to others. Nor will our continuing celebration of violent power, whether political, economic, military, or religious—a particular problem in the United States—contribute much to the creation of such a world. Only images of communities of reconciliation—in which all recognize that they are "members one of another," as Paul put it (Rom. 12:5), with no discrimination among groups, classes, races, or genders—can focus our attention and our lives on the commitments we today must make, and the loyalties we must maintain, if we are to align ourselves with those cosmic and historical forces pressing us toward a more humane world. In this context of hopes and dreams the image of the self-sacrificial Jesus, who gives himself completely—and nonviolently—so that all might have "abundant life" (as John 10:10 puts it), stands out in its full significance. Here is a vivid emblem of the radical transvaluation of values that is required if our world of violence and aggressive self-assertion is ever to become more truly humane and thus more human. The earliest Christians believed they had been called by God to just this sort of healing and reconciliation, and they believed that it was the power of the divine spirit working among and within them—the power, that is, of those evolutionary and historical momentums (to use the language of this book) that are moving in the direction of a more truly humane world—that led them to respond affirmatively to that call. This reconciling and healing power, imaged in and symbolized by Jesus and the early Christians, continues to call men and women today to respond to the need for, and to the forces working toward, such reconciling activity in our world. With these momentous stakes in mind, I propose this reconstruction of the conceptions of God, humanity, and the world (much too briefly sketched here) as providing a way for Christian faith—and perhaps some other faiths as well—to reconstitute themselves in light of our contemporary evolutionary/ecological sensibility and knowledge.

It is obvious, I presume, that the transformation of faith envisioned here is not likely to come about easily or soon, though it is clear that women and men not infrequently make changes in the faith-structures out of which they have lived (that is, religious conversions occur) and such changes are always going on in times like our own. Probably only rarely, however, are such changes brought about simply by deliberate decision, for these matters lie deep in our selfhood and in our religious and cultural values, commitments, and practices. However, those who find themselves profoundly dissatisfied with their present stance in life and the world often discover ways to make some deliberate moves toward alternative postures. People can, for example, decide to move permanently into a culture or religion significantly different from the one in which they were originally socialized, fully aware that this will change their world, their life, their values, and meanings in decisive, unforeseeable ways; one can deliberately make a vocational decision that will drastically change one's whole way of life, and the values and meanings that had informed one's life up to this point, and so on. So changes of different sorts and of diverse degrees can in fact be made in our ways of living, our value commitments, our meaning-understandings, our basic faith-stances—by individuals and also by communities—if attractive options become available.

In this book I am trying to make visible such an option for Christian faith, for Christian orientations in life and the world. Many Christians today, formed to deep levels by traditional understandings of the basic Christian symbols, may find this option unsatisfactory and will pass it by. There are some, however, who will (I have reason to believe) find this way of thinking about Christian faith and life to be liberating, indeed saving. Instead of continuing to despair about reconciling their deep Christian commitments with their modern/postmodern sensibilities and understandings of human existence in today's world, such persons and groups may find the suggestions I am presenting helpful, as they work their way through to a compelling and challenging version of their faith.

On Thinking of God
as Serendipitous Creativity

I n the previous chapter I proposed *serendipitous creativity* as a metaphor more appropriate for thinking of God today than such traditional image/concepts as creator, lord, and father. In this chapter I shall elaborate more fully and nuance more carefully that concept. It is no longer possible, I contend, to connect in an intelligible way today's scientific, cosmological and evolutionary understandings of the origins of the universe and the emergence of life (including human life and history) with a conception of God constructed in the traditional anthropomorphic terms. However, the metaphor of creativity—a descendant of the biblical concept of creation, and directly implied in the idea of evolution itself—has resources for constructing a religiously pertinent and meaningful modern/postmodern conception of God. In this chapter the notion of creativity is explored with respect to the profoundly serendipitous mystery implied in it; its usefulness in orienting human life today, particularly in connection with contemporary ecological issues; and its implications for such traditional theological themes as the problem of evil and "God is love." The chapter concludes with a brief characterization of what human life and faith would be like if ordered in relation to a God conceived as serendipitous creativity instead of a God defined in the more traditional anthropomorphic way.

Biblical texts (as was noted in the prologue) have been the most influential source of Christian and other Western thinking about God. When those texts were written, the earth and its immediate environment (the "heavens") were regarded as all that existed, the universe. And though this universe was doubtless immense to the humans living within it, it was minuscule by today's standards. In that historico-cultural situation it was not implausible to imagine some almighty personal being who existed before and apart from the universe and by all-powerful fiat brought it into being (as in Gen. 1). Moreover, one could imagine this superpersonal being taking up clay from the ground and forming creatures, including humans, out of it (see Gen. 2). Both of these types of creativity were well known at that time, and it is not surprising, therefore, that humans imagined the universe being brought into existence through acts of this sort. The biblical stories thus supplied an account of an ultimate origin of things and of an ultimate personal power behind all things—God—that still remains plausible to many.

In my view, however, we can no longer continue thinking of God along these lines. What could we possibly be imagining when we attempt to think of God as an all-powerful personal reality existing somehow before and independent of what we today call "the universe"? As far as we know, personal agential beings did not exist, and could not have existed, before billions of years of cosmic evolution of a very specific sort, and then further billions of years of biological evolution also of a very specific sort, had transpired. How then can we today think of a person-like creator-God as existing before and apart from any such evolutionary developments? What possible content can this more or less traditional idea of God have for those of us who think of the universe in our modern evolutionary way, according to which no life or consciousness can be imagined apart from the emergence of these very specific and quite extraordinary conditions?[1]

The idea of creativity, however (in contrast with the notion of a creator)—the idea of the coming into being through time of the previously nonexistent, the new, the novel—continues to have considerable plausibility today; indeed, it is bound up with the very belief that our cosmos is an evolutionary one in which new orders of reality come into being in the course of exceedingly complex temporal developments.[2] In my view, therefore, those interested in theological reflection and construction can and should continue to work with the idea of creativity, but they should no longer think of this creativity as lodged in a *creator-agent* (a concept no longer intelligible). There are a number of advantages to this move, though it also presents us with some serious ambiguities and problems.[3] In this chapter I reflect on some of these, thus elaborating further and nuancing in certain respects what was sketched in chapter 1 about God as creativity.

I

First, let us consider briefly some features of the idea of creativity itself. It might be assumed that creativity is to be thought of as a sort of force at work in the cosmos, bringing the new into being. Some of the rhetoric in my writing and speaking (including within *In Face of Mystery* [Kaufman 1993a]) may suggest this. This sort of thinking in effect just substitutes the notion of force for God, implying that creativity is simply a kind of *im*personal—instead of personal and agential—power. To make that sort of claim, however, presupposes that we know more about the emergence of truly new and novel realities than we actually do. But the notion of creativity itself carries a strong note of mystery. It differs from "mystery" in that it directs attention to the coming into being of the new, whereas "mystery" (when used in a theological context) refers to fundamental limits of all human knowledge (Kaufman 1993a, 54–69) and carries no such further meaning. But creativity is profoundly mysterious; as the ancient phrase *creatio ex nihilo* (creation out of nothing) emphasized, the coming into being of the truly new and novel is not something that we humans understand. We can see this most vividly, perhaps, when we consider the old unanswerable question, Why is there something, not nothing? As Nicholas Berdyaev put it, "Creation is the greatest mystery of life, the mystery of the appearance of something new that had never existed before and is not deduced from, or generated by, anything" (1937, 163). To regard creativity as a kind of "force" is to suggest that we have a sort of (vague) knowledge of an existing something-or-other when in fact we do not. All we really see or understand is that new and novel realities have begun to exist in time. There is a serendipitous feature in all creativity: more happens than one would have expected, given previously prevailing circumstances, indeed, more than might have seemed possible (Kaufman 1993a, 279).[4] In the case of evolving life we see that this occurs through chance variation and selective adaptation, but neither of these can properly be reified into "causes" or "forces" (in any ordinary sense of those words) that directly *produce* the new creation. Creativity *happens*: this is an absolutely amazing mystery—even though we may in certain cases, for example with the evolution of life, be able to specify some of the conditions without which it could not happen.[5]

Precisely because of this close connection with the idea of mystery, "creativity" is a good metaphor for thinking about God. If used properly, it preserves the notion of God as the ultimate mystery of things, a mystery that we have not been able to penetrate or dissolve—and likely never will succeed in penetrating or dissolving. This aspect of the notion of creativity draws us into a deeper sensitivity to God-as-mystery than some of our religious traditions do, with their talk of God as *the Creator*. For this latter concept seemed to imply that we knew the ultimate mystery (God) was really a person-like, agent-like being, one who "decided" to do things, who set purposes and then brought about the realization of those purposes—as a potter or sculptor creates artifacts (Gen. 2) or as a poet or king brings order and reality into being through uttering words (Gen. 1). Absent these models of creativity, the biblical writers might never have generated their radical notion of creation, eventually to be elaborated in terms of the formula of *creatio ex nihilo*. With Darwin, however, we have learned that significant creativity can be thought of in other ways as well. Indeed, according to evolutionary theory these human models of agential creativity themselves came into being ("were created") as cosmic processes in the course of long stretches of time brought into being certain very complex forms of life. The most foundational kind of creativity for us today, therefore, appears to be that exemplified in the evolution of the cosmos and of life, rather than that displayed in human purposive activity. Though we can describe the evolutionary model with some precision, it in no way overcomes the most profound mystery at the root of all that is: Why is there something, not nothing? Why—and how—can the new actually come into being in the course of time? Nor does the Big Bang throw any light on these questions; it only succeeds in raising them over again in an extremely acute form.[6]

Thinking in terms of the ultimacy of the mystery of life and the world in this way is in keeping with the concern of the tradition of negative theology (see prologue, section V) that we not reify God in any way, that we not think that we really know what or who God is (for example, an anthropomorphic agent who makes covenants with us, takes care of us in special ways, etc.). God is, in the last analysis, utterly unknowable. As the German hymn writer Gerhard Tersteegen (d. 1769) put it: "A God comprehended [that is, successfully captured in, and thus mastered by, our human concepts and images] is no God."[7] Pseudo-Dionysius, Maimonides, Thomas Aquinas, Eckhart, Luther, and others all understood this, though unfortunately they often compromised this insight by claims about special "experiences" of God or "revelations" from God (which, of course, gave humans a sense of profound knowledge, comfort, and certainty). In the view I am presenting here, these compromises are no longer made: God is utter mystery, the mystery of creativity; speaking of God as creativity in no way diminishes the ultimacy of the mystery with which life confronts us.[8]

The metaphor of creativity, as I have been suggesting, is appropriate for naming God because (1) it preserves and indeed emphasizes the ultimacy of the *mystery* that God is, even while (2) it connects God directly with the coming into being—*in time*—of the new and the novel.[9] I highlight the significance of this second point by calling attention to the serendipitous aspect of creativity, a matter of special import when we attempt to think of God in this way. Humans, of course, are (so far as we know) the only beings that can or do take note of the creative processes and events in the world and who believe that apart from these processes we—and all else that makes up the world—would not exist at all. Only humans, therefore, are in a position to value the creativity in the world, and particularly to value its serendipitous character. If we value our own existence, we can hardly fail to regard as serendipitous the continuous coming into being of the new that has led to the emergence of humankind through a highly beneficial (for us) though a quite surprising and chancy sequence of events. We would not exist had there not been a quite particular succession of happenings, summarized by astrophysicist Martin Rees as follows:

> For life like us to evolve, there must be time for early generations of stars to have evolved and died, to produce the chemical elements, and then time for the Sun to form and for evolution to take place on a planet around it. This takes several billion years. . . . The size of our universe shouldn't surprise us: its extravagant scale is necessary to allow *enough time* for life to evolve on even one planet around one star in one galaxy. This is an example of an "anthropic" argument, which entails realizing that the Copernican principle of cosmic modesty should not be taken too far. We are reluctant to assign ourselves a central position, but it may be equally unrealistic to deny that our situation in space and time is privileged in any sense. We are clearly not at a typical place in the universe: we are on a planet with special properties, orbiting around a stable star. Somewhat less trivially, we are observing the universe not at a random time, but at a time when the requirements for complex evolution can be met. (1997, 229–230)[10]

It is thus quite appropriate to remind ourselves from time to time of the serendipitously creative character of the specific trajectory of the cosmic evolutionary process that produced us humans. Characterizing our trajectory in this way—and thinking of God in terms of the metaphor of serendipitous creativity—are further examples of what (as Rees suggests) has come to be called *anthropic* thinking. That is, these examples call our attention to a feature of the universe that is of special importance to us humans, and they *name* this feature in a way that points out its significance not only for us humans but also for our understanding of the universe as a whole. These ideas are not merely of subjective human interest and import: they tell us something that is also objectively true of the cosmos within which we live. The symbol "God" has always functioned in this way to call attention to that reality believed to be of greatest importance for ongoing human life, and in this respect it is an anthropic idea (though it need not be an anthropomorphic idea, as I argue throughout this book). The concept of serendipitous creativity can perform a similar anthropic function in relation to our modern/postmodern cosmological thinking, and for this reason I regard it as providing a useful way to bring the symbol "God" into significant connection with that thinking.[11]

II

In our use of the word "God," we humans are attempting to direct attention to what can be called the "ultimate point of reference" of all action, consciousness, and reflection. No regressive reflection seeking to push back to an ultimate starting point, no creative action moving toward an unstructured future, no appreciative feeling of worship or devotion expressing the orientation of the whole life of the self can intend some reality "beyond" God (Kaufman 1995, 14). But the idea of an ultimate point of reference is itself much more abstract than the concept of God. What more, then, should be said? In *In Face of Mystery* (Kaufman 1993a) and in this book I have taken the position, following suggestions of theologian H. N. Wieman, that God should be thought of as creativity; creativity is the only proper object of worship, devotion, and faith today, the only proper ultimate point of reference for our valuing (as was argued in chapter 1). Everything other than the ultimate mystery of creativity is a finite created reality that may indeed be valued and appreciated within certain limits, but which is itself always subject to distortion, corruption, and disintegration and thus must be relativized by the creativity manifest in the coming into being and the ultimate dissolution of all finite realities—that which alone may be characterized as "ultimate."

There is a problem here, however. Creativity understood as the coming into being of the new whenever and wherever this occurs—new evils (as we humans understand them) as well as new goods—raises some difficult questions. (On this issue I depart significantly from Wieman, for whom the "creative event" is always "the source of human good.") The biblical God, of course, was thought of as sometimes bringing into being what from our human perspective appear to be great evils, as well as goods: "Does evil befall a city, unless the Lord has done it?" asks the prophet Amos (3:6); "I make weal and create woe," says Yahweh through the mouth of Isaiah (45:7; see also Job, Jeremiah, and many other texts). In the New Testament, for the most part, God's fearful judgment and destructiveness remain despite the theme that "God is love" (as 1 John 4:8,16 put it). God is a frightening judge and destroyer as well as a forgiving father and redeemer; in this both Old Testament and New were consistently monotheistic. Thinking of God as serendipitous creativity—a mystery beyond our comprehension—is also consistently monotheistic.

However, if one takes this sort of position, can serendipitous creativity be regarded as always manifesting what is ultimately valuable for humans, a norm to be followed in all situations? Are we humans to emulate God's destructivity, God's bringing evils (as they seem to us) into being, as well as goods? These ideas may raise serious questions for Christians as well as others, although those who have regarded the warrior metaphor as apt for God (and Christ) have in the past been willing to draw these conclusions. For those who take a radically *christomorphic* faith-stance,[12] however, the creation of horrific evils can hardly be regarded as appropriate human activity. This concern has become particularly important today, when the human project can no longer tolerate the destructiveness of unrestricted warfare, for we now have the power to bring all human life (as well as much other life on planet Earth) to a halt. Clearly creativity without qualification—creation of historical trajectories going in almost any direction—cannot be regarded as a norm appropriate or helpful for the guidance of human life and activity: our human creativity, in accord with the normative christomorphic images, stories, and ideas in the New Testament, must be directed toward bringing goods into the world, not evils, toward healing, toward resolving disputes through compromise and mediation, toward overcoming the destructive momentums we humans have already brought into the ecological order on planet Earth and into the historical order of human affairs. The human creation of trajectories of massive destructiveness must be put out of bounds. But how can qualifications of this sort be reconciled with the claim that cosmic serendipitous creativity should be regarded as the ultimate point of reference in terms of which human existence is to be oriented, ordered, and normed?

This is not an insoluble issue. Problems arise here only if we think of serendipitous creativity in the abstract, as that creativity manifesting itself throughout the cosmos in trajectories of many different sorts, some of them in sharp tension with others.[13] However, when we consider that humans are neither responsible for nor can do much about most of what goes on in the universe, we can see (remembering the christomorphic principle) that the examples of creativity that are to be regarded as normative for us must be restricted to the *productive creativity* manifest on *planet Earth and its immediate environment. Earth and its environment* is really the only region of the cosmos that can be affected by our actions and projects (at least for the foreseeable future), and it is within this context that we must, therefore, seek to understand both our place in the created order and the activities appropriate for us to engage in; *productive creativity* alone is fitting, for clearly there is no reason to suppose that we humans have been in some way "authorized" (by an abstract cosmic creativity) to engage in extensive destruction of life and its ongoing momentums, which have taken thousands of millennia to emerge. Such a claim would manifest monstrous hubris and arrogance.

Thus, we must be quite constrictive in our thinking about our projects and our creativity: it is on a particular biohistorical trajectory that we humans have come into being,[14] and it is this trajectory that serves as the niche in Earth's ecological web where we must live and act. Doubtless this trajectory will end at some future time, but there is no basis for arguing that it is our proper human business to bring that about: our creativity, rather, should be exercised in searching out ways to live within our ecological niche on this planet, with a minimum of destructiveness of the other lines of life that also have their homes here. This is the moral implication of our growing ecological sensitivity and consciousness in recent decades: we no longer can live basically concerned with only the human project; our knowledges and sensitivities today enable us to understand that our project needs to fit much better into the broader ecology of planet Earth than often heretofore. It is our task today, therefore, to make whatever creative moves we can that will facilitate this. This does not mean that all destructive activity must be ruled out for humans; indeed, we need to destroy many of our own present patterns of action, ways of thinking, institutions, and so on, if we are to succeed in creating ecologically appropriate forms of human life on planet Earth. But destructiveness of this sort will be in the service of the further creative movement of the biohistorical trajectory that has brought us into being and continues to sustain us. Thus our creativity will be serving—rather than restricting or otherwise countering—the forward movement into the open future on planet Earth of the cosmic serendipitous creativity to which we seek to be ultimately responsible. In this way, the seeming paradox involved in regarding cosmic serendipitous creativity as the ultimate point of reference for our human devotion, thinking, and action dissolves away. Attempts to employ this ultimate mystery abstractly as a norm for making judgments about concrete cases here on Earth will always be obscure and dubious, as were attempts in the past to invoke "God's will" directly as justification for particular human decisions and actions.

These considerations bring us into a position from which we can take up briefly some further concerns that Christians might have respecting the proposal that we think of God as serendipitous creativity. Consider, for example, the Christian affirmation that "God is love" (1 John 4). In many respects this notion represents the epitome of Christian anthropomorphism/anthropocentrism. Do the theological moves I am advocating rule out or make unintelligible this central Christian claim? The fundamental anthropomorphism of Israel's God-talk (as displayed in the Old Testament) helped prepare the way for using the metaphor "love" as the defining characterization of God in Christian thinking and practice. Because loving, caring attitudes and behaviors are of such importance in human life, thinking of God in terms of this metaphor had—and still has—great rhetorical power: God, the very creator of the universe, is seen here as standing in an intimate loving relationship with every person, God is "our father in heaven" who will meet every human need. "Even the hairs of your head are all numbered," as the words of Jesus put it (Matt. 10:30). Thus both the deep human longing for unlimited *agape-love* and an exceedingly powerful way of addressing that longing found significant realization in the conception of God as loving. The basic anthropomorphism of the early Christian conception of God made this thought seem both plausible and saving.

Does the move to a de-anthropomorphized God (as I am proposing) require us to jettison this whole way of thinking? No, it does not. What it does require is that we think through carefully the way this human need for love is to be understood in relation to serendipitous creativity. As we have been noting, it would certainly be a mistake to argue that cosmic creativity always manifests love for all the creatures involved: that would be unintelligible, indeed absurd, in face of all we know about nature "red in tooth and claw," to say nothing of the apparent origins of the universe in a Big Bang conceived in fundamentally physicalist terms. But there is every reason to maintain—in the theological position I am sketching—that the emergence of the love that has become of such central importance to human being and well-being must itself be seen as connected to the creativity that brought into being our humanity. In the processes through which our humanness was created, activity and attitudes and behaviors of the sort we call "loving" came into focus; love emerged with the human creatures who could respond to it. In our corner of the universe—that is, on the trajectory that has brought humans into being—capacities and needs for *agape*-love gradually became important and prized (at least in some quarters). So in and through our specifically human relation to God (as Christians have claimed), loving, caring attitudes and activities have become a significant feature, and love is both given and received—unlike the relations of creativity to many other spheres of the cosmic order, each of which has its own distinctive character.[15]

It would, of course, be improper to say simplistically and without qualification that "God is love," as Christians have sometimes done in the past; that would be to project on every feature and dimension of the universe what we find to be true and highly significant (only?) in our distinctively human sphere. But it is far from improper to say that not only in our relations with other humans, but also in our human relation to God (creativity) and in God's relation to us, *agape*-love has become an important feature. In that sense, we can still say, "God is love," although this is not the only way in which God should be characterized, nor is it the most fundamental or defining metaphor to use in thinking of God. That place must be reserved for the serendipitous creativity universally manifest. Of course Christians have always understood that a whole configuration of terms must be used in characterizing God ("power," "omnipresence," "eternity," "creativity," and so on), not "love" alone; indeed, to try to conceive God simply and completely in terms of the metaphor "love" would make both God and that metaphor unintelligible.

A brief word should, perhaps, be added here about the implications of all this for the concept of *evil*, a notion central in a number of religious traditions. I have argued elsewhere that this concept, and the correlative concept of salvation from evil, are generated largely by concerns about our own human well-being and fulfillment, on the one hand, and about human disaster or failure, on the other:

> The framework of valuation here is [as Spinoza argued] anthropocentric—at least initially. . . . The acts of generalization that occur as these complexes of terms are developed [in monotheisms], however, move toward transcendence of their anthropocentric origins. . . . And with the conception of God— though the name "God" initially designated, perhaps, that reality believed to be ultimately salvific of the human—there is clearly an attempt to indicate a point of reference in terms of which all else (including, of course, the human itself) can be assessed and judged. . . . [I]n radical monotheisms . . . the original awareness of evil as bound up with one's own pain and destruction [may become] completely concealed or even reversed (as in, for instance, the Calvinist triumphant willingness to be "damned for the glory of God"). (Kaufman 1996a, 87–89)[16]

Thus, though having its biological roots in the adverse response of living organisms to pain, the theological notion of evil in monotheistic traditions actually moved far beyond all anthropocentrism to the creation of a trans-human criterion for judging everything human: all human behavior, motivations, actions, institutions, and so on, were to be assessed in light of what God was thought to will and require (however good or bad that might seem to humans); living in faith came to be understood as involving the attempt to order all of life in terms of these divine requirements. Our human-centered judgments about right and wrong, good or bad, were overruled with the emergence of theocentric faith: what God *is* doing and what God *wills* for humanity became the ultimate criterion in terms of which all judgments of value and goodness, truth and meaning, were to be made; centering life on any other reality than God was idolatrous.

Obviously, these ideas can be connected fairly easily with the theological position sketched in this book. Indeed, conceiving God as serendipitous creativity—thus moving away from the anthropomorphic/anthropocentric tendencies in much traditional thinking—makes the theocentric feature of our God-talk more emphatic and austere than in most traditional views, and this is accomplished here (as just noted) without losing sight of God's loving relationship with humankind. The cosmic serendipitous creativity manifest throughout the universe is taken to be the ultimate criterion of all value and meaning, but the application of that criterion to our actual human living and dying cannot be made in these abstract terms but must be made, rather, in terms of the facticities of our human situatedness in the evolutionary/historical trajectory that has brought about and continues to sustain our human existence on Earth. Any human acts or practices, customs or institutions, that violate or are otherwise destructive of the biohistorical constraints within which humankind must live and work are to be characterized as "evil"; in contrast, whatever creatively facilitates the forward movement of the evolutionary/historical trajectory of which we are part—and is in relative harmony with the wider ecological order on Earth—is to be considered good, right, fitting.

Judgments made about values and meanings, about good and evil, continue here to have a direct bearing on and pertinence for human being and well-being, but they are no longer governed by essentially anthropocentric criteria. Because they are basically concerned with the ongoing sustainability of human existence within the web of life on planet Earth, they have a certain ecological objectivity—however difficult it may be, in specific cases, to ascertain in scientifically measurable terms just how this is to be conceived. "Evil" and "good," therefore, cannot be properly considered as merely a function of human desires and wishes.[17]

III

Let us step back now and take note again of the enormous difference in scale of today's vast universe as compared with the biblical one in which human God-talk began. The universe that we must take into account today—as we attempt to think about God and our obligations in the world—did not come into being just a short time before humanity was created. Nor does it consist largely in what is visible to the naked human eye; most of it appears to lie beyond the reach of even our most powerful telescopes and other instruments. Thus, both temporally and spatially this universe is of an entirely different order than anything imaginable by humans through most of history. Women and men have existed in this universe for only a minuscule fraction of its temporal development, and human activities and actions can have effects only quite locally on planet Earth and its immediate environment. Our place in God's universe and our responsibilities in God's world must thus be understood as much diminished from what our traditional stories and images suggest.

God also (and God's "eternity")—if God is to be thought of as the creativity manifest in the ongoing evolution and development of this entire vast cosmos (thus continuing a central theme of the monotheistic religious traditions)—will have to be conceived as much greater in scale and in mystery than anything suggested by the stories and images that informed and constituted most traditional thinking. The kind of personal intimacy with God fostered by many of these images—especially such anthropomorphic ones as "father," "lord," and "king"—no longer seems appropriate, or even imaginable or intelligible. So our human "relationships" with God will have to be conceived in much vaguer and less vivid terms than in the piety of the past—the characterization of God as serendipitous creativity straightforwardly suggests this—and our understanding of human existence as "under God" will be experienced as much more open, much looser, much less determinate and specific. Life no longer will be thought of or experienced as dependent on our unmediated direct relation to a divine

being whose character and will, and whose requirements of the
human, are fairly clear and distinct. Rather, we must come to understand that how we live out our lives and take responsibility for ourselves and our activities here on planet Earth are matters that we
humans ourselves must work out as carefully and responsibly as we
can[18]—*normed* of course (as we have noted) by the directions in which
creativity appears to be moving in our part of the cosmos and by the
christomorphic principle. Thus, our lives and our ethics—all of the
matters bearing on how we live and think and act—will have to be
oriented much more in terms of the overall context of human life here
on Earth than traditional ways of thinking about God and our relation to God have suggested. Earth is our home, and it should no
longer be said or thought that we are "strangers and foreigners on the
earth . . . [who] are seeking a homeland . . . a better country, that is, a
heavenly one" (Heb. 11:13, 14, 16).

Our modern/postmodern world-picture, taken together with the
conception of God as serendipitous creativity, evokes a significantly
different stance in the world than that associated with the Christian
symbol-system as traditionally interpreted. The childlike trust and
assurance and consolation, characteristic of the conviction that
throughout our lives we are cared for lovingly by a heavenly father, are
no longer available. In exchange, we humans become aware of ourselves as a unique species deeply embedded in the magnificent intricate web of life on planet Earth, with distinctive obligations and
responsibilities to that web and the creativity (the coming into being
of the new and the novel) manifest in it—creativity present and active
throughout the cosmos and in all human cultural and religious traditions and activities. Thinking of God as creativity undercuts the arro-
gant stance of much traditional Christianity vis-à-vis the natural
order as a whole, as well as with respect to other religious and secular
traditions. Christians may no longer consider themselves to be
authorized in what they say and do by God's special revelation.

Nevertheless, important continuities with traditional Christian
understandings remain, continuities significant enough to warrant

considering this picture of God, the world, and the human as appropriate for Christian faith today. As was noted in chapter 1, understanding the ultimate mystery of things, God, in terms of the metaphor of serendipitous creativity manifesting itself in a variety of evolutionary and historical trajectories—instead of in terms of the anthropomorphic creator/lord/father metaphors that constituted the traditional picture of a God with largely anthropocentric purposes—facilitates (more effectively than did the traditional imagery) maintaining a decisive qualitative distinction (though not an ontological separation) between God and the created order. This distinction is the basis for regarding God (serendipitous creativity) as the *sole* appropriate focus for human devotion and worship, as that which alone can properly orient us in the world. All other realities, being created goods that come into being and pass away, become dangerous idols that can bring disaster into human affairs when worshiped and made the central focus of human orientation. To attempt to order one's life in terms of this important distinction between God (the ultimate mystery of things) and the idols, can only be, of course, a move of faith, of a deep trust in the mystery that has brought us into being and continues to sustain us. As biohistorical beings that have emerged on one of the countless creative trajectories moving through the cosmos, humans are indissolubly part of the created order and not in any way to be confused with the creativity manifest throughout the cosmos, in all its complexity, order, and beauty. We can exist only (as far as we are aware) within the boundaries and conditions of life found on the particular trajectory within the created order in which we have appeared.

Though strikingly different in important respects from some traditional Christian emphases, this understanding of God and of the human is clearly a form of *radical monotheism* (to use H. R. Niebuhr's term). As we have seen, it is a conception that can be developed into a Christian interpretation of human faith and life, if the creativity that is God is brought into significant connection with the poignancy and power of the stories and character of Jesus and the early church. The reconstructions of the conceptions of God and humanity suggested here thus provide a way for Christian faith to reconstitute itself in respects appropriate to our contemporary evolutionary/ecological sensibilities and knowledges.

Humans did not bring the world into being, and it is not we who sustain it. We did not create the evolutionary process, forever bringing into being new, unforeseeable forms of life. There is a powerful, awe-inspiring creativity manifest in our world—and indeed, in ourselves: the new, the novel, the unforeseeable, the previously unheard of, break forth roundabout us and in our midst; and human life continues to be sustained from beyond itself. This serendipitous creativity provides grounds for our hope for the future. Human life can go on and, we dare to hope, will go on. And we are called to participate ever more fully and effectively in the creative transformation of our existence that will enable this to happen.

chapter three

In the beginning . . . Creativity

et us begin this chapter by recalling the paraphrase of the opening verses of the Gospel of John with which this book began: "In
the beginning was creativity, and the creativity was with God,
and the creativity *was* God. All things came into being through the
mystery of creativity; apart from creativity nothing would have come
into being."

As was pointed out in chapter 2, creativity is a mystery that we
humans cannot understand and behind which we cannot go.
Through our concepts of causation we are able to understand various
processes of transformation, of change, in things that already exist.
But mere change is not what we mean by the word "creativity," for
changes can generally be understood and often explained, and they
do not involve the coming into being of something truly novel. The
concept of creativity in no way explains how or why new realities
have come into being; rather, it simply gives a name to the profoundly
mysterious fact that novel realities have come into existence in the
course of time. As the ancient phrase *creatio ex nihilo* suggests, the
coming into being of the truly new—the totally unexpected, the

utterly inexplicable—is not something of which we humans are in a position to make sense.

In our Western religious traditions the coming into being of the new has generally been thought of as brought about by God. And to say that God—thought of as some kind of personal being that has existed from eternity—has created everything does seem to give a kind of explanation of the existence of the world and its contents. But how is this to be understood? According to Genesis 1:3, "God said, 'Let there be light'; and there was light." God said this, and God said that, and all these things immediately sprang into being. We can imagine such events as magical happenings of some sort, but we have no actual experience of events of this kind (though a distant partial analogy may be seen in the work of a poet or potter, as the writers of Genesis saw); therefore we really have no way to understand what these words mean. Although they evoke some specific images and ideas, we are left with the sense that we are saying something quite important though very vague and unclear: we do not know what it is that we are saying. In the biblical account God's creative activity is not confined to the origin stories of Genesis. Rather, from time to time, God continues to bring into being new realities: "They are created now, not long ago; before today you have never heard of them" (Isaiah 48:7). Paul refers to Christians as "new creations" (2 Cor. 5:17), and in Revelation we are told that God is going to "make all things new" (21:5) at some future time. All of these claims, of course, are completely unsubstantiated belief. It is our familiarity with the biblical account, and with the basic idea of God as omnipotent Creator of all things, that leads us to suppose that we understand what we are saying when we utter these words. But in fact we cannot grasp the idea of creation, of something coming from nothing. This remains for us a profound mystery.[1]

What, then, are we to make of the paraphrase of the opening words of the Fourth Gospel with which this chapter began: "In the beginning was creativity, and . . . [this] creativity was God"? Two quite different interpretations come to mind. In the ordinary understanding of John's Gospel, it is usually assumed that to say "the Word was God" (1:1) is a declaration that the Word (which a few verses later will be identified with Jesus) is fully divine. John goes on to emphasize this point immediately by stating, "All things came into being through" this Word (1:3); this is what created the heavens and the earth. Were we to follow this pattern of interpretation, my paraphrase would be redundant, simply asserting that the "creativity" that brought all things into being is nothing other than the activity of the creator—and we would be left with our familiar ideas about both God and creativity. The other interpretation of the paraphrase, however, turns this all around and asserts that the phrase "creativity was [or is] God" is not redundant at all but rather a claim about what our word "God" designates: it is *creativity* that is God; when we use the word "God," it is the profound mystery of creativity to which we are referring, and it would be a mistake, therefore, to let the familiarity of our personalistic images and ideas of God get in the way of our recognizing the significance of this point. The word "creativity," as we have been noting, leaves the question of how or why the new comes into being completely open, and (in this second interpretation) the word "God" is the religious name for this mystery that goes beyond human understanding. This interpretation implies that we should beware of unconsciously importing any images or ideas—personalistic or other—into our thinking about God, for that would be refusing to acknowledge the ultimacy of God's (creativity's) profound mystery, instead of facing up to what that mystery means for us. It would be claiming we know something that we cannot possibly know, why and how there is something and not nothing.

In the Genesis 1 story, although the created realities spoken of there—like the sun and moon, plants and animals and humans—are all things that we know perfectly well, just what the creator God is, or how and why God is able to bring these sorts of things into being, remains completely unexplained. It is interesting to note that (as we shall see) the modern story of the Big Bang, the subsequent coming into being of the cosmos, and the eventual evolution of life has similar limitations: all that we actually see or can understand here is that new realities have emerged in the course of time. In this account, like in the biblical account, the how and why of creation remain profound mysteries. We should not allow ancient religious assumptions and beliefs to lead us into thinking we know or understand what happens in events or processes of this kind. God, of course, has always been understood to be a profound mystery, but the way in which God has been talked about has often involved fudging this point and proceeding as though we knew that God is really a personal being, one of enormous power who can create at will things that previously did not exist. Thinking of God as *creativity* (rather than as "the Creator") forces us to take the profundity of God's mystery to a deeper level. For "creativity" is simply a name with which we identify this profound mystery of new realities coming into being; it is in no way an explanation of it.

What has come into being is the whole vast cosmos—with all its multifarious contents—the wide context of our human lives. Within this developing cosmos, after billions of years of further creativity,[2] life emerged on planet Earth and gradually evolved along many different lines (as we have today come to believe); on one of these trajectories, after further billions of years of creativity, mammals, primates, and finally humans came into being. This particular development represents, of course, only one line of the creativity manifest in our universe, but it is the one that—in its serendipitous superabundance—brought humans into being and thus is of special meaning and importance to us. To become aware of this awe-inspiring mystery of creativity is to come out of the dark unconsciousness of these matters—within which most of life, and of human history as well, has existed—into the paradoxical consciousness and knowledge of the profound mystery within which we humans live. It is this mystery of creativity, I am suggesting, that we today should think of as *God*.[3]

I

What does it mean to think of God as creativity, to think of creativity as God? What is creativity? What do we know about creativity? With what kind of conception of God does this notion provide us? How is the mystery of God illuminated by this identification? The events and processes that have brought the universe, with all its enormously fascinating and diverse features, into being are today subjects of scientific inquiry; and during the last century a new overall world-picture addressing these questions has been developed and is now widely accepted as the best understanding of these matters that we humans have. In this chapter we will look at the basic outlines of this picture with a view to uncovering what (if anything) it may tell us about creativity—and thus, about God. I am not an expert in any of the scientific fields drawn upon here; I rely upon more or less popular accounts by scientists (and commentators on the sciences) for the material I am examining. I have tried to set out views on which there is fairly wide agreement among scientists, but on some points, I may have strayed down false paths. Especially in my discussion of the newly emerging "complexity theory"—important for my argument but also quite contentious—I may have made some moves that better-informed persons would regard as questionable. But I hope that the basic picture that I present here will prove illuminating—at least for theological purposes—despite its scientific shortcomings.

It is important to acknowledge right at the outset that "creativity" is not a word much used by scientists. This may be because it has such wide potential application. Since it focuses attention on the coming-into-being of something new or novel, it can be employed with reference to almost anything, to everything—and thus it is difficult (perhaps impossible) to define and specify it with the strict conceptual and experimental controls so important in scientific work. However, precisely this comprehensiveness of application enables this term to be useful theologically and philosophically, for it encourages us to focus on and hold together in a single concept a very significant feature of life and the world, namely that novel realities continuously come into being in time—an insight that, back into ancient times, has been understood as of central theological significance. The concept of *creativity*, thus, enables us to connect important theological concerns with central features of modern/postmodern thinking about the cosmos, the evolution of life, and the emergence and biohistorical development of human life and culture on planet Earth.

As a framework for thinking about what we might mean by this word, I suggest that we examine three significantly different modalities of creativity, each of them involved in mystery in its own distinctive way; putting this point theologically, one can say that creativity (God's activity) will be considered here in connection with three different contexts, and thus in three different forms. The first of these modalities—which I shall call $creativity_1$—has already been briefly discussed: the initial coming into being of the universe in which we find ourselves, sometimes expressed as the creation of something from nothing (*creatio ex nihilo*). In trying to understand this baffling idea, it is worth asking ourselves why and how we humans create ideas of this sort—and that will direct our attention to a quite different modality of creation that I will label $creativity_3$, human symbolic creativity. We will also need to consider the creativity manifest in evolutionary processes, the ongoing coming into being of trajectories of increasingly complex novel realities. In this mode creation is not thought of as simply and straightforwardly from nothing (as often with $creativity_1$); it is, rather, creation in the context of other realities that already exist—$creativity_2$, we shall call it, the kind of complex processes that today are believed to have produced, in the course of some billions of years, humans (as well as many other creatures). $Creativity_2$ provides (among other things) a link between $creativity_1$ and $creativity_3$. There are, doubtless, other ways of thinking about the concept of creativity, but this three-fold division enables us to view it from three distinctly different angles.

The ideas of the Big Bang and the subsequent evolution of the world and of life have become commonplace today, features of a very comprehensive way of thinking that some commentators believe is increasingly bringing the sciences back into relation with each other as they now proceed with their work.[4] After some years of vigorous debate a widespread consensus appears to be developing among cosmologists about the basic facts of the universe—how old it is, how large it is, the various stages through which it developed, and so on.[5] It is believed that the universe is very large indeed, perhaps consisting of as many as 200 billion galaxies, each of which, on average, likely contains 100 billion stars (Rue 2000, 51). The universe is thought to have begun in what is commonly called a Big Bang, now believed to have occurred 14 billion years ago (Overbye 2002). Since we often use numbers to specify with some precision what we are talking about, we may tend to overlook or forget the layers of profound mystery in the story these particular numbers set before us. I cannot go into detail on this, but I would like to mention a few points here.

Scientist Stephen Hawking tells us that "At the big bang itself, the universe is thought to have had zero size, and . . . to have been infinitely hot" (Hawking 1988, 117). Though this may be plausible mathematically, it is very difficult to imagine or think just what is being said here about an actual state of affairs: what could it mean to describe this whatever-it-is as of "zero size" (cf. *creatio ex nihilo?*), and how could anything of that sort be the beginning of our "universe"? What could the phrase "*infinitely* hot" mean? These puzzles, of course, belong only to the beginning point of everything, but with the Big Bang the universe immediately started (we are told) to expand at an enormous rate. What can it mean to say that something of zero size is "expanding"? In all of these expressions some of the words are used in very nearly unintelligible ways; at best, we seem to be dealing here with a mystery that cannot be articulated clearly in our ordinary speech. Let us continue:

> As the universe expanded, the temperature of the radiation decreased. One second after the big bang, it would have fallen to about ten thousand million degrees . . . about a thousand times the

temperature of the center of the sun. . . . At this time the universe would have contained mostly photons, electrons, and neutrinos . . . together with some protons and neutrons [these all being infinitesimal particles of which atoms are made]. . . . About one hundred seconds after the big bang, the temperature would have fallen to one thousand million degrees, the temperature inside the hottest stars. At this temperature protons and neutrons . . . would have started to combine together to produce the nuclei of atoms of . . . heavy hydrogen . . . which contain one proton and one neutron. . . . [These] nuclei then would have combined with more protons and neutrons to make helium nuclei. . . . Within only a few hours of the big bang, the production of helium and other elements would have stopped. And after that, for the next million years or so, the universe would have just continued expanding, without anything much happening. (Hawking 1988, 117–19)

Stop for a moment and think about each of the items in this picture. Though verbally intelligible, they are scarcely conceivable or imaginable: more mystery here—though Hawking assures us that "We are fairly confident that we have the right picture at least back to about one second after the big bang" (Hawking 1988, 118). Now all of this about which we are speaking is, of course, only *our* universe. However, as Dennis Overbye, a science writer, says, some theorists think that "the universe we see, the 14 billion light-years, is just a tiny piece of a much vaster universe, or even a whole ensemble of them, forever out of our view" (2002, D6).

We have already noted difficulty in grasping individual details of this picture. Let us consider now the picture as a whole. It is hardly imaginable or thinkable: a picture of a tiny, enormously hot speck of some sort ("of zero size") which—for no reason at all—suddenly blows up in a huge Big Bang that produces, in the course of just a few hours of almost inconceivably rapid inflation, the beginnings of what we might properly call our universe. It is important to emphasize that we have no way of knowing whether there was anything before the Big

Bang or, if there was, what it could have been. Nor can we know anything beyond our universe, that "vaster universe" or "ensemble" of uni-
verses which, as Overbye says, is "forever out of our view." So all of this
remains utter mystery. Hawking explains why: our "universe has a
beginning and an end at singularities that form a *boundary* to space-
time . . . *at which the laws of science break down*" (Hawking 1988, 139;
emphasis mine; see also 122, 133, and 136).[6]

According to this statement, scientists have discovered the Big
Bang and the subsequent development of the universe through exceedingly ingenious imaginative application of the so-called laws of science,
and we can, therefore, have considerable confidence in this picture.
However, the story is somewhat more complicated than that. For
where did these "laws of science" come from? As we shall see in a
moment, there is a good deal more mystery of creativity here than
Hawking's account suggests. For now, however, we can see that the Big
Bang is for contemporary science a boundary where these laws "break
down," and therefore no knowledge of what has brought it about can
be attained. If Hawking's claims are correct, we have arrived at what
appears to be one of the unsurpassable limits of all human knowledge
of our world as we know it. Thus, we and our universe are ensconced
in inscrutable mystery on all sides—though it is claimed, of course,
that we know a great deal in considerable detail (through "the laws of
science") about the development of our universe beginning immediately after the Big Bang. It is important that we note that the Big Bang
is not regarded as an atomic event with no significant connection to
anything before or after: though we cannot know anything about what
might have preceded the Big Bang, its effects—what follows upon it—
are cumulative and long-lasting (but probably not unending) as new
structures and patterns gradually emerge in the universe that is coming into being. These forms of order and ordering then become the
contexts within which further creative activity (that I suggest we call
creativities$_{2,3}$) occurs. And this further creative activity also cumulates
and develops and brings more new forms of order into being through
long and increasingly complex creative evolutionary processes.

However impressive may be our knowledge of the consequences of the Big Bang, we have no way of finding out anything about how or why the Big Bang itself occurred. "This means," as Hawking says paradoxically, "that one might as well cut the big bang, and any events before it, out of the theory, because they can have no effect on what we observe" (Hawking 1988, 122).[7] The Big Bang, thus, really gives us no answer at all to our question, Why is there something, not nothing? All we can say is that the enormous creativity obviously occurring in and with the Big Bang is a complete mystery—a mystery *to us*: we are at the limits of our knowledge here. But this does not mean that there was nothing before the Big Bang, or that there was no context of any kind at all within which the Big Bang occurred. It means that we humans have no way—and quite possibly will never have any way—of learning why or how the Big Bang occurred. We are in no position to say that the Big Bang is a preeminent example of "something coming from nothing" and we can have no way of knowing how this great originative event came about. This is all utter mystery.

II

The mystery with which we are involved here goes deeper than has thus far been considered (though this is not often taken up in the scientific accounts). Where did this somewhat fantastic story about a Big Bang—this "singularity," as the scientists call it—come from? Everything I have sketched (and there are many details that I have omitted) has been worked out carefully and painfully by scientists here on Earth—on this second-rate planet going around a third-rate sun in one of the billions of galaxies in our universe. This whole story has been built up in connection with careful observations of data all found here on planet Earth or its immediate vicinity. These observations have been studied and refined for generations, during which more and more convincing interpretations and explanations have been developed, and these involved increasingly elaborate and ambitious creative extrapolations beyond planet Earth and beyond all human experience. These highly imaginative extrapolations from our human position here in the twenty-first century extend, on the one hand, far backward in time—at least as far back as 14 billion years ago—and they include many temporal periods that came into being and passed away long before there were any living inhabitants on planet Earth, indeed before this planet existed. On the other hand, these extrapolations move unbelievably far out in space—14 billion light-years in all directions, very far away indeed from the planet on which they were created, refined, and developed.

Extrapolations of this sort—based upon and thus including the accepted interpretations and explanations of the pertinent data found here on planet Earth—are all, of course, human *imaginative constructions*.[8] They have been created by the power of the human imagination (creativity$_3$) to pull together into a coherent and intelligible picture (by means of its interpretations and explanations) observations and data from many disparate sources. Why and how did this enormous human imaginative power come into being? How reliable are its extrapolations and other constructions that are the basis of all our cosmological knowledge? We are confronted once again with profound mystery, in this case the mystery of the creativity that has produced our human imaginative and cognitive powers—creativity$_2$, taken together to some extent (as we shall see) with creativity$_3$—as well as the mystery of the degree to which those powers are reliable. The imagination has created innumerable sets of symbols—images, noises, marks on paper—and symbol-systems; these (at least some of them) are regarded as standing for the so-called "realities" of life and the world about which we seek to learn. (The symbol "God"—my principal concern in this book—and the symbol-systems in which it has been of central importance are, of course, also among these creations of the human imagination [see Kaufman 1995, especially chapter 2].) How and why did humans begin to create this whole new world of symbols? To put this question in theological terms: How are we to understand the divine creative activity—working transformatively (creativity$_2$) within the context of the already created world—as now transmogrified somehow into the modality of creativity$_3$ and manifesting itself in and through the self-conscious human imagination? If we think of God as creativity (as I am proposing), we have an important example here of what was traditionally spoken of as the indwelling of divine spirit in our human spirits; but how is this to be understood?

We can, of course, give a historical account of this development. From very early on humans have found it useful, indeed necessary, to picture to themselves—that is, to *imagine*—the environment in which they lived; to create, that is to say, images and ideas of the setting in which they found themselves. Without such pictures, stories, and ideas it would have been impossible to act—to think about the future, make plans for that future, and then carry through those plans in the best possible manner. Many of the more ancient of these pictures and myths, however indispensable they were to the peoples who created them and lived within the terms they provided, seem to us fanciful today, even quite absurd. That is because we are heirs to thousands of years of imagining, reflecting upon, and experimenting with a great variety of these world-pictures and have gradually devised ways of critically testing them—largely through meditation, reflection, and tentative experimentation, and then more fresh imagining. In the last three or four hundred years some of these activities have become increasingly disciplined and convincing, as the methods of modern science were gradually developed and employed. But it remains profoundly mysterious why and how all of this development (of creativity$_3$) has occurred. What we are seeing in our exceedingly complex, carefully argued, and highly imaginative modern cosmological and evolutionary thinking is one of the outcomes to date of this long history of human attempts to understand what kind of beings we are, what kind of world we live in, what our rightful place in that world is, what are the ultimate realities and powers with which we humans must come to terms. Along with that search the slowly developing, somewhat surprising, indeed perhaps ultimately inexplicable mystery of human symbolic creativity has come into being serendipitously (more about this below).

Since all these world-pictures and myths—from the most primitive to the most highly sophisticated, whether deeply religious or thoroughly scientific or both—are creations of the human imagination, none may be regarded as revealing some kind of final truth about humanity and the world: all are fallible human symbolic products and must be subjected to ongoing critical examination. One of the most important features of modern scientific methods is that a kind of continuous critical scrutiny and questioning of the concepts, proposals, and conclusions that are being developed has, with some success, been built into them. But all such critical examination—since it is always carried out by men and women here on Earth—is itself fallible, however "creative" it might be. And perhaps, as a consensus begins to form on issues long in dispute—as may be happening now in modern cosmological science—one should hesitate about getting too quickly on the bandwagon.

I am not trying here to discredit in any way modern cosmological and evolutionary theory: it is, in my opinion, by far the best thinking we have about our world and our human place within the world. And therefore it is appropriate to live and think and act in the terms with which it provides us. But at the same time we should take up a thoroughly critical stance. Our awareness, that these modern pictures of an unimaginably great and ancient cosmos are all grounded in exceedingly ambitious human imaginative extrapolations from data here on our tiny planet in a remote corner of the universe, should lead us to recognize the fragility of these ideas. This is the best picture we have—a grander and more fully articulated vision of the world than any before it. It has been produced by the power of the human imagination to create symbols and symbol-systems (creativity$_3$)—a truly amazing mystery; nothing of this sort (as far as we know) had existed before humans came on the scene, or exists independently of our human activity. In the future these symbolic constructions will doubtless change and develop in ways now completely unforeseeable (as has frequently happened historically).

In sharp contrast with the creativity through which the massive universe, in which we now take ourselves to be living, came into being (creativity$_1$), many different worlds of signs and meanings—*languages* in innumerable fantastic variations—have come into being through our (partly conscious, perhaps largely unconscious) human symbolic creative activity. The countless sorts of ideas and images; memories and hopes; fears and anxieties; achievements and failures; ways to live and act; societies and cultures of many different kinds; imaginary worlds (in the literary arts); forms and patterns and designs of all sorts (in the plastic arts); vast worlds of music and mathematics and dance; theories and hypotheses of many quite diverse philosophies, sciences, and religions; innumerable meanings of all sorts; and connected with all of this the terrifying experiences of meaninglessness—none of this would exist apart from this creativity$_3$. Nothing like this enormously prolific symbolic creativity is to be found in the story of the Big Bang; indeed, that story itself is a product (as we have just been noting) of creativity$_3$, as articulated in modern mathematics and the modern sciences. Symbolic creativity came rather late into the world (beginning perhaps some hundreds of thousands of years ago), as human beings slowly emerged partly in and through the gradual creation of language. This latter development helped to bring about the growth of the large prefrontal cortex that distinguishes our human brains from all others, as brain scientist Terrence Deacon has argued (see below). As our remote ancestors came out of Africa and gradually spread around the globe, human linguistic developments, and along with them other forms of human symbolic and cultural creativity, moved in many different directions. Obviously we cannot trace all these developments here, but they are the background without which the accelerating imaginative creativity that began to appear four centuries or so ago—the creation of all the many complex sides of the modern world, and in the course of that the creation of the modern sciences and technologies—cannot be properly understood.

The mystery of this creativity$_3$—though very different from the mystery of the Big Bang—is surely as striking and as important to humans as those earlier mysteries that it apparently presupposes (creativities$_{1,2}$). Indeed, as we have noted, it is only through our human symbolic activities that the story of those earlier mysteries was itself created. Those earlier creativities$_{1,2}$ produced the material and vital orders of the world in which we live, and this later creativity$_3$—appearing in and through the activities of our human minds, our spirits, and producing the whole mental/spiritual world—is itself an emergent outcome of those prior modalities of creativity. This seems to suggest that creativity should not be thought of as a static reality, always and everywhere the same, but rather as itself modulating and developing in ways appropriate to the increasing complexity of the realities it is producing and within which it appears. (The theological implications of this point will be discussed below in section V.) Descartes and his followers thought of *mind* and *matter* as two absolutely distinct types of reality, and it is not difficult to understand why they took that position. But this claim has become increasingly problematic. Darwin's idea of evolution was the most important factor in this change, for it provided a way of thinking how mind could have emerged in the course of the evolution of the material and vital orders here on planet Earth. Evolutionary theory has now become (as noted above) the great all-comprehensive picture that integrates the highly diverse features of our universe under one grand concept.

Creativity$_3$ appears to be a special complexifying of creativity$_2$ (to be discussed in a moment). Before and apart from it, there would have been no symbols or symbol-systems, no symbolic creativity, no symbolic worlds. It was "the co-evolution of language and the brain," as brain-scientist Terrence Deacon has argued, that made possible the creation of these symbolic realities found only in human cultures.[9] In human symbolic activity (when it is fully in place) creativity becomes for the first time self-conscious and deliberate. With the emergence of language humans became capable of naming and imagining a variety of goals toward which their actions could be directed; that is, the capability of imagining and naming matters that were not in fact present in their experience became for the first time self-conscious and deliberate. This made choice among alternative objectives possible, and with it the beginnings of planned courses of action to realize those objectives. In and through all of this, human culture was created (not deliberately and consciously, of course, but coincidentally—a very serendipitous coincidence indeed!) as humans learned how to make, use, and talk about such things as tools and other desirable implements, garments to protect against the cold, and (perhaps most important of all) how to produce food—the invention of farming. (See the discussion of creativity$_2$ below, especially the portion of section IV that draws on Gerd Theissen and Jared Diamond.) Gradually humans became aware that they were able to use to their advantage not only things at hand like sticks and rocks and animal skins: they were able to deliberately design and make new objects that would be useful in their day-to-day living. That is, creativity$_3$ was coming on the scene. But how was this creativity$_3$ itself *created*, if humans were not able to imagine it first? It was creativity$_2$—in the mysteriously serendipitous aspect that creativity sometimes manifests—which gradually produced the conditions enabling human self-conscious life to emerge. Creativity$_2$ has, of course, continued to affect historical developments in important ways even though deliberate human decisions and actions have come to have their own powerful creative consequences (see Kaufman 1993a, chapters 19–22).[10] So what we have in creativity$_3$ is a blend of a continuing serendipitous creativity$_2$ with the more recently emerging self-conscious and deliberate human creative activity that is made possible by linguistic (and other) symbols and symbol-systems.

III

Let us now turn to creativity$_2$. We obviously cannot explore all the manifestations of this modality of creation (given the exceedingly complex evolutionary picture that the modern sciences present today), but it will prove illuminating for us to look a bit at how the creative evolutionary development of the world and of life may have come about. We left the story of the beginnings and early development of the cosmos with Hawking's observation that shortly after the Big Bang the universe began rapid expansion lasting "for the next million years or so." Here is Loyal Rue's description of the latter part of that early expansion and what followed:

> For several hundred thousand years the universe remained too hot for nuclei [of atoms] to succeed in capturing electrons. But when conditions were right [sic] copious amounts of hydrogen and helium atoms began to form, and for the next billion years or so the universe billowed forth in an expanding cloud of cooling gas. The organization of matter had commenced. . . . [After another] billion years or so, . . . the gaseous universe began to fragment, . . . and then gradually reorganized into separate clouds, each moving away from all the rest. These fragmented clouds—over 100 billion of them— were destined to become galaxies. The process of galaxy fragmentation was completed by the time the universe was . . . 5 billion years old. (2000, 57)

Scientists have uncovered some very interesting and surprising details about this expansion. As Hawking puts it, "If the rate of expansion one second after the big bang had been smaller by even one part in a hundred thousand million the universe would have recollapsed before it ever reached its present size" (Hawking 1988, 121-22). And, as Rue continues, "if the explosive force [of the Big Bang] were any greater (or the gravitational force . . . any less), . . . the universe would have expanded more rapidly than it did—too rapidly for any galaxies or stars to form" (2000, 62). Deeply mysterious features of the processes creating our world continue to appear!

What more needs to be said here about the mystery of creativity$_2$, the creativity manifest in the continuing cosmic evolution and eventual emergence of life? As was noted in chapter 2, Martin Rees has summarized briefly what had to happen before complex forms of life could emerge:

> For life like us to evolve, there must be time for early generations of stars to have evolved and died, to produce the chemical elements, and then time for the Sun to form and for evolution to take place on a planet around it. This takes several billion years. . . . The size of our universe shouldn't surprise us: its extravagant scale is necessary to allow *enough time* for life to evolve on even one planet around one star in one galaxy. (1997, 215)

Other details about these developments are quite surprising:

> The laws of science, as we know them at present, contain many fundamental numbers, like the size of the electric charge of the electron and the ratio of the masses of the proton and the electron. . . . The remarkable fact is that the values of these numbers seem to have been very finely adjusted to make possible the development of life. For example, if the electric charge of the electron had been only slightly different, stars either would have been unable to burn hydrogen and helium, or else they would not have exploded. . . . It seems clear that there are relatively few ranges of values for the numbers that would allow the development of any form of intelligent life. Most sets of values would give rise to universes that, although they might be very beautiful, would contain no one able to wonder at that beauty. (Hawking 1988, 125)

One can see why many continue to argue that there must have been some sort of intelligent "Designer" behind this whole creativity$_2$ process. But others, trying to understand this creativity in naturalistic terms, suggest that the increasing complexity itself—which was gradually emerging in the world at large and later developed especially in living organisms—can account for the novel realities that in due course appeared. In most of our thinking (scientific and otherwise) we seek to simplify what we observe and are considering, and as a result we are often satisfied with misleading explanations of things. So when the matters with which we are dealing are in fact exceedingly complex, we may easily misunderstand what is happening. According to the new theories of complexity that are now appearing, it was the gradual growth, over billions of years, of increasingly complex organizational patterns themselves—first, in galaxies and stars, atoms and molecules—that eventually made possible the emergence of life; the increasing complexity of life then gradually brought into being the countless forms that have evolved, including those forms that have become conscious, thoughtful, imaginative, and responsible agents—humans.[11] Understanding the importance, thus, of this growing complexity and how it works should significantly illuminate creativity$_2$. Philosopher/theologian Mark C. Taylor, in his recent book *The Moment of Complexity: Emerging Network Culture* (2001), explores and critically reflects on some of the remarkable ideas and theories about complexity and its creativity, which are now being discussed by physicists, mathematicians, evolutionary biologists, philosophers of culture, and others. These ideas provide a conceptual apparatus that will give us a greater sense of the profound mystery of the ongoing creativity in the world and in life. Early in his book, Taylor presents an overall picture of this sort:

> According to complexity theorists, all significant change takes place *between* too much and too little order. When there is too much order, systems are frozen, and cannot change; and when there is too little order, systems disintegrate and can no longer function. . . . According to [Ilya] Prigogene disorder does not merely destroy order, structure, and organization, but is also a condition of their formation and transformation. New dynamic states . . . *emerge* in conditions far from equilibrium. . . . Complex adaptive systems . . . always emerge at the edge of chaos . . . [and] are in a state of continual evolution. (2001, 14–15; emphasis mine)

It is this complex interactive intermix of order and disorder in all systems, structures, and organisms, sometimes coming to the very "edge of chaos"—this inextirpable intermix of "information" and "noise" (to use the more technical terms in which these analyses are often expressed)—that is the womb within which new forms may be created. Taylor explains:

> There can be no information without noise and vice versa. Noise can no more be silenced in the world than parasites can be exterminated. . . . "Mistakes, wavy lines, confusion, obscurity are part of knowledge," [Taylor quotes Michel Serres as saying,] "noise is part of communication." . . . When programs are flexible and codes adaptable, noise can be processed in ways that allow *novelty* to emerge. . . . The emergence of the new reconfigures the old in unexpected ways that allow differences not previously articulated to emerge. . . . Noise becomes "responsible for the growth of the system's complexity" [Serres]. (2001, 121–122; emphasis mine)

These are startling and puzzling words. Creativity is here presented as somehow emerging—mysteriously, without explanation—between the order and the disorder, the information and the noise, found in every system or structure. It is this mysterious creativity that is somehow intimately involved with the evolution of the cosmos from the Big Bang to the complex universe we know today; it is this mysterious creativity that is particularly manifest in the unfolding of life on planet Earth. Serres notes that an organism is "a hypercomplex system. . . . This system is not in equilibrium, since thermodynamic stability spells death for it. . . . It is in a temporary state of imbalance, and it tends as much as possible to maintain that imbalance. It is . . . subject to the irreversible time of the second law, since it is dying. It struggles against time" (quoted in Taylor 2001, 135).

"Life," Taylor sums up, "continues only as long as things are *out of balance*" (135). Moreover, the evolutionary dynamic of life develops from relatively simple into innumerable highly complex forms. One reason we humans have found it so difficult to understand creativity is because we have all too often thought of nature as in a kind of harmony, a balance; but that is a mistake. All systems are in some respects *out of balance*, and sometimes—at the "tipping point" as it is called—the present order gives way to a new better-adapted order, and creativity has occurred. On other occasions the existing order simply breaks down in chaos at the tipping point and is destroyed. The tipping point is that instant when what had been ordinary "quantitative change suddenly leads to qualitative change" (Taylor 2001, 148).

> "Complex behavior in nature," [Per] Bak argues, "reflects the tendency of large systems with many components to evolve into a poised 'critical' state, way out of balance, where minor disturbances may lead to events, called avalanches, of all sizes . . . catastrophic events rather than . . . a smooth gradual path. The evolution of this very delicate state occurs without design. . . . The state is established solely because of the dynamical interactions among individual elements of the system: [it] . . . is *self-organized.*" . . . In the state of self-organized criticality, nonlinear events can have effects disproportionate to their causes. . . . The dynamic interactions . . . generate global events that require a holistic description, which cannot be reduced to an account of the individual elements. Finally, at the tipping point, the effect of individual events is unpredictable. (Taylor 2001, 148–149)

The important points for us to note here are the following: (1) All complex systems, structures, and organisms have an internal organization that holds them together and makes them precisely *this* system or organism. This feature is not imposed from without but is a kind of *self-organization.* (2) This internal self-organization is always in tension, in certain respects *out of balance.* (3) Though it can never be predicted just when or why a *tipping point* will come, when it does come, an *avalanche* with quite unpredictable consequences follows. (4) These consequences may be completely destructive, with the earlier order breaking down into chaos, or they may have self-organized into a new pattern, better adapted to the environment than the old one—the creation of a novel reality, a reality that had not existed before. What we have here is a general description of creativity$_2$; what we don't have is an explanation of how or why precisely this or that novel reality has come into being through this process. Creativity$_2$ of the new is always unpredictable, unexpected, surprising; it can be described in some detail, but not fully explained. Taylor sums up this picture of organized systems and evolution in these words:

> Emerging self-organizing systems are *complex adaptive systems*. For complex systems to maintain themselves, they must remain open to their environment and change when conditions require it. Complex adaptive systems, therefore, inevitably evolve, or, more accurately, coevolve [with their environment]. As the dynamics of evolving complexity are clarified, it not only becomes apparent that complex adaptive systems evolve, but . . . that the process of evolution is actually a complex adaptive system. (2001, 156)

These ideas—out of balance, tipping point, self-organizing systems—give us a way to think about creativity$_2$, creativity in the world of nature. Although there is no way of applying these ideas to the Big Bang (since we can know nothing about conditions before and surrounding it), they are applicable to cosmic and biological evolutionary development, including the period of rapid expansion. Descriptions of this sort, of course, do not imply that the mystery in these developments has now been dissolved away. At present we know very little about how and why and when the crucial evolutionary tipping points occurred; and even if we were to learn much more about these matters, it is doubtful this would explain in any adequate way their creative outcome. We do not (and may never be able to?) understand the mystery of how greater and more complex things can come out of simpler and lesser things—the version, appropriate to creativity$_2$, of the old question asking why there is something and not nothing. None of these descriptions and quasi-explanations, it should be noted, give us any real knowledge of the future toward which this whole creative process may be moving—not of the fairly immediate future, or the ultimate future of the human project on planet Earth, or the future of the universe as a whole. (Of course scientific extrapolations that present the sun's burning out, an ultimate recollapse [or expansion and dissipation into virtual nothingness] of the whole universe, and so on, have been, and doubtless will continue to be, made.) Does creativity (God) go on forever whether the universe dies or not? As we have been noting, we can reconstruct in and with our imaginations a vague and general picture of the course in our universe of creative activity to date—from the Big Bang through cosmic evolution, the evolution of life, and the emergence of history and historicity; but creativity itself—God—never becomes visible in our extrapolations. From our present standpoint it seems likely, therefore, that God (if God is thought of as creativity) may remain profound mystery forever.

IV

We have now filled out a little further the notion of creativity$_2$. It is not possible to sketch here the extraordinary complexity of the full evolutionary story. However, to round out the overall picture under construction in this chapter, it is important that we consider further the momentous transition through which the emergence of creativity$_3$—our own human creative activity in the world—may have come into being (was created). Let us, then, explore briefly the way in which the emergence (within the evolution of life) of human history and historicity may have occurred. Two considerations will be taken up: (1) the emergence of human history and historicity largely through the development of language and culture, and (2) the emergence and development within history (in some historical streams) of what Jared Diamond, a professor of physiology, calls "autocatalytic" processes.

Taking for granted the importance of the coevolution of language and the brain (briefly discussed above), let us consider the later stages of the process through which we human beings, as we think of ourselves today, may have been created. As noted in chapter 1, section II it has been especially through our *historical* sociocultural development over many millennia—not our biological evolution alone—that we humans have acquired many of our most distinctive characteristics. Our increasingly comprehensive knowledge about the natural world in which we live, for example, has provided us with considerable powers over our immediate environment on planet Earth, and over the physical and biological (as well as sociocultural and psychological) conditions of our existence, powers that go far beyond those of any other animal. As we saw, it is *qua* our development into beings shaped in many respects by historico-cultural processes of this sort—that is, humanly created, not merely natural biological processes, our *historicity*—that we humans have gained these increasing measures of control over the natural order, as well as over the onward movement of history.

This is no small change, to be regarded as just one more of the many unique developments that have appeared as the evolutionary process has meandered down its many distinctive lines. This is an enormous qualitative change in the evolutionary process itself, an "evolution of evolution," as Gerd Theissen, a scholar in the study of religion, has called it (Theissen 1985). In the emergence of history and historicity within the evolutionary process, all the "decisive factors in evolution—variation, selection and preservation—change" (17).

> What happened unconsciously in pre-cultural evolution, the furthering of life through selection (which always means suffering), becomes *conscious* in human beings: the dull suffering of creation finds a representative voice in [humans]. (30; emphasis added) The effect of culture is to *reduce* [natural] selection . . . [for] culture is able to make life possible even where nature would drastically diminish its chances. (46; emphasis added) Religion . . . the

heart of human culture . . . is a rebellion against the principle of
selection. It makes human beings open to a greater reality. (49) [In
culture, more] important than the increase of genes is the preservation of values, norms, insights, and forms of life in which genetic
rivals work together in co-operation. . . . Through religion human
beings succeeded in identifying themselves with their non-genetic
fellows, treating them as though they were kinfolk, indeed part of
themselves. . . . [Through their] capacity to make and transfer
symbols, human beings have been able to take that small step
beyond previous evolution which allows them to have inklings of
a freedom from the power of genetic and social egoism. . . . As cultural beings they see themselves exposed to the demand of fur-
thering life through an increasingly comprehensive solidarity with
those very people who are the losers in the fight for the distribution of opportunities. (142–45)

The growth of human cultures (and, correspondingly, of human
symbolic behaviors) has affected significantly (as we noted) the
actual biological development of the predecessors of today's *homo
sapiens*, including the evolution of our brains (Deacon 1997). The
gradual in-building of complex culturally-created dimensions and
processes into our human nature has meant that creativity$_3$—
humans, over many generations, creating in history new forms of
humanity—has been as indispensable a factor as biological evolution
(creativity$_2$) in bringing today's humanity into being. Only within the
order of human history have beings appeared with self-consciousness, great imaginative powers and creativity, freedom and responsible agency.[12] (Although some of the "higher" animals show signs of
some similar powers, they are far from developing the complex symbolic and cultural worlds that have enabled humans to transform
themselves as well as the face of planet Earth.) In and through millennia of proto-historical developments (in concert with continuing
biological evolution) human biohistorical existence came on the

scene. Beings with great symbolic facility (creativity$_3$), beings with capacities to imagine the counter-factual (what is not present in experience, indeed, what never has been nor will be experienced, a veritable infinitude of possibilities),[13] beings with *historicity*—these did not appear, thus, simply as the last stage of what had hitherto been a strictly biological process; it was a biological process (creativity$_2$) becoming increasingly blended with historical features (creativity$_3$). Thus (as we saw in chapter 1), all the way down to the deepest layers of our distinctly human existence, we are biohistorical beings, beings decisively shaped by our historicity,[14] itself an emerging product of our emerging creativity$_3$.

We humans are, thus, as anthropologist Clifford Geertz put it, "incomplete or unfinished animals who complete or finish ourselves through culture—and not through culture in general but through highly particular forms of it: Dobuan and Javanese, Hopi and Italian, upper-class, academic and commercial" (Geertz 1973, 49). Each of these particular cultures, though interconnected with the others in its environment, has come into being through its own particular history (creativity$_3$), a history that has, in quite distinctive ways, shaped it and its values and meanings, its institutions and practices, its ways of living and dying, and thus shaped the very selves of its people. The human historical project from early on has been thoroughly pluralistic. Some of these diverse historical strands became highly dynamic, giving birth to massive cultures and societies of great complexity and creativity, producing artificial worlds within which human life was carried on. Others have remained much closer to the world of nature. The sharp disparities among our many diverse cultures seem now, however, to be breaking down in some respects. Modern science and technology, which had their beginnings in the growing dynamism of Western culture several centuries ago, have now spread around the world and are actively pursued and creatively practiced in most of today's more complex civilizations. They (along with many other factors) are becoming an intellectual and institutional force increasingly promoting (creativity$_3$) global interaction, intercommunication, and structural interconnection.

Why and how have some historico-cultural processes become so highly dynamic and creative, increasingly dominating the globe?

This brings us to my second point, the development, within some historical streams, of what Jared Diamond calls "autocatalytic" processes. In our reflection on the emergence of human biohistorical existence up to this point, we have focused for the most part on the importance of the invention of language and other forms of symbolization that made it possible for humans to live within symbolic worlds—always reshaping and transforming the given world of nature, and (sometimes) facilitating the emergence of further fruitful human creativity. But why, in some historical strands, has this historicity developed into enormous cultural productivity, increasingly becoming global, while other less dynamic strands are either swallowed up in this powerful movement or simply left behind? Though I have argued that all human societies are biohistorical and are distinctively shaped (creativity$_3$) by their specific historicities, the particular conception of human historicity with which I am working here—emphasizing its potential for powerful dynamism and creativity—has been drawn largely from what we see and experience in the modern/postmodern societies and cultures in which many of us happen to live. (It is important, of course, not to forget the similar creativity and dynamism to be seen in a number of the great civilizations of the past.) Diamond points out that much of life in the hunter-gatherer stage of human existence—although made possible (as we have noted) by the beginnings of language and well developed brains much like our own—was largely ordered by basic biological needs; this, by itself, was not enough to get "autocatalytic processes" (as he calls them) going in history. An autocatalytic process is "one that catalyzes itself in a positive feedback cycle, going faster and faster once it has started" (Diamond 1997, 111). Without processes of this sort getting under way in our history, we would not be the particular kind of biohistorical beings that I have been suggesting we now are increasingly becoming.

According to Diamond it was, above all, the human movement into deliberate food production (8500–7500 BCE) that enabled this self-accelerating process to begin (100). Once a larger and more reliable food supply was readily available, enough leisure time was assured so that societies could begin to differentiate into diverse crafts and other groupings, each concerned with certain specific tasks and skills through which they could become inventive and productive (creativity$_3$) in new ways. The political order also changed, and societies became more hierarchical in character. They could, thus, be mobilized to tackle new problems: warriors, for example, who could capture goods and slaves from outside groups, could be trained, and in various ways a much more complex sociocultural order gradually emerged. It *emerged*: it was definitely not planned by anyone but is an example in early stages of human history of what I call the "serendipitous creativity" manifest in the world (Kaufman 1993a, chapter 19 and following chapters; see also footnote 10, above). The development of food production was the site in which this change first began to occur, and without which it might never have appeared at all (Diamond 1997, 110–12).

> What actually happened was not a *discovery* of food production, nor an *invention*, as we might first assume. There was often not even a conscious choice between food production and hunting-gathering. . . . The first people who adopted food production could obviously not have been making a conscious choice or consciously striving toward farming as a goal, because they had never seen farming and had no way of knowing what it would be like. . . . Food production *evolved* as a by-product of decisions made without awareness of their consequences [serendipitous creativity]. . . . However, once food production had arisen in one part of a continent, neighboring hunter-gatherers could see the result and make conscious decisions. (105-108)

> In all parts of the world . . . archaeologists find evidence of rising densities [of population] associated with the appearance of food production . . . [which is] an autocatalytic process. . . . A gradual rise in population densities impelled people to obtain more food. . . .

> Once people began to produce food and become sedentary, they
> could shorten the birth spacing and produce still more people,
> requiring still more food. . . . The much denser populations of food
> producers enabled them to displace or kill hunter-gatherers by their
> sheer numbers. . . . In areas where there were only hunter-gatherers
> to begin with, those groups . . . who adopted food production out-
> bred those who didn't. (111–12)

Thus a natural biological selection process gradually favored the food
producers, and they had the additional bonus of the unplanned development of increasingly complex sociocultural forms of life. An autocatalytic historical process was getting under way serendipitously, a
process through which human life, and the face of the earth, would be
completely transformed. Humans were becoming thoroughly biohistorical beings.

We have come, by this point, to the kind of history with which we
are familiar: a history of varieties of communities and institutions;
social and cultural practices; moral codes and forms of life; ways of
thinking and acting; diverse crafts and skills; much struggle within
human populations and among various human groups; a history of
human conscious and self-conscious activity; deliberate setting of personal and social goals; reflection on life and its meaning or meaninglessness; development of diverse forms of religious activity; deliberate
study and speculation about the world about us and the nature of
human life within that world; a history in which human imagination
and reflection is becoming well-developed and consciously cultivated; a
history within which human creativity therefore is manifest at many
points; a history in which there is much humanly created evil as well as
many goods. Humans have become, in every dimension of their lives,
biohistorical beings, the kind of beings capable of creating (creativity$_3$)
the modern sciences and their world-pictures (along with all the rest of
our modern highly complex human existence). It is important to note,
of course, that no individual or society planned all these creative developments and then carried them through. Though human creative

activity was at every point present, much of what developed was neither foreseen by anyone nor deliberately brought about by human endeavors. These great historical creations were the serendipitous product of the autocatalytic momentums that had begun to emerge in and through creativity$_2$ and continued to unfold in and through creativity$_3$.

V

In the course of this chapter—concerned with sketching what it means to regard God as *creativity*, and thus creativity as *God*—we have explored briefly three "modalities" of creativity, three distinctly different settings in terms of which we can focus on the coming into being of all things novel in our world. Creativity$_1$—creativity in an absolutist form (so to speak), in its total inexplicability and its questionable intelligibility—is exemplified in the contemporary picture of the origins of the universe, the Big Bang. Why and how the Big Bang occurred cannot be known because this event (if it can be properly regarded as an "event") is itself an unsurpassable limit of our knowledge; our scientific laws are thought to break down here, and we have, therefore, no way of learning what could have "caused" this event to happen (if the notion of cause can be properly invoked here). So all we have is profound mystery—the naked and unadorned mystery of something coming into being (from nothing). Nevertheless, the Big Bang is a very important concept in contemporary cosmological theory—a fact that, of course, deepens even further its mystery. [15]

Creativity$_2$ and creativity$_3$ are in some respects more readily intelligible than creativity$_1$, since we know something of the contexts within which they occur, and we are able, therefore, to specify some of the conditions without which they would not have been possible. But we do not know how or why they can be creative. Neither of these is an unqualified *creatio ex nihilo*, though both exemplify features analogous to that,[16] and both remain deeply mysterious in many ways, as we have been noting. Creativity$_2$—following on the Big Bang in a 14-billion-year exceedingly complex development—appeared within the enormous expansion and eventual proliferation of cosmic and biological evolutionary trajectories. In the course of time, billions of realities of countless different types and sorts came into being on these trajectories. Current complexity theory provides a way to think about some features of these developments, but this understanding is just the tip of an iceberg, most of which still remains hidden from view. The mystery of creativity$_2$, as we are able to think of it today, is obviously very wide and comprehensive and deep.

How creativity$_3$—human symbolic and cultural creative activity, eventually leading into self-conscious and deliberate creation of count-less cultural/symbolic forms, realities, and worlds—could ever emerge out of creativity$_2$ is also a profound mystery, a mystery connected with the emergence of humans as self-conscious and responsible biohistori-cal beings. It seems likely that without the distinctive coevolution of language and the human brain that occurred on planet Earth, this could never have happened; but much remains unknown. In any case, without the emergence of self-conscious beings like ourselves, with our powers of symbolic creativity, this whole picture of the developments from the Big Bang onward would never have been created.

Where does this leave us? If we think of God as creativity, cre-ativity as God, what does this examination of creativity tell us about God? Creativity (God)—the coming into being of the new, the novel—as we have noted, is to be found everywhere we turn: from the Big Bang through the cosmic expansion into galaxies in which stars and planets emerge, through the appearance of life on planet Earth and its evolution into countless forms, ultimately including biohistor-ical beings in which creativity becomes to some extent self-conscious and deliberate. That is, God (creativity) apparently is always and everywhere active in some degree and some respect—a theologically momentous conclusion. In all of this, it should be clear, God is to be distinguished from everything created. And yet, creativity$_3$ seems to be in certain respects a creation of creativity$_2$: as creativity continues to manifest itself in a world of growing complexity, it transmogrifies itself in ways appropriate to that development. God's activity, though always *creative*, apparently changes (and grows?) in time in distinctive ways appropriate to the context in which God is acting. And thus God also apparently grows and changes.[17] The theological implications of this are vast.

It is important to note that the three modalities of creativity in this analysis are dialectically interconnected with each other: we cannot think clearly about any of them without thinking of them all in their interconnection. Together they provide a sketch of the creativity in the universe (as seen from and thought about on planet Earth in the twenty-first century), a creativity that seems to be itself growing in its potential and grandeur. All that is being said here is, of course, itself a product of creativity$_3$: it is a structure of symbols. The ideas of the Big Bang (creativity$_1$) and of the 14-billion-years-long evolutionary path (creativity$_2$) from the Big Bang to symbolic creativity are themselves symbol-systems (products of creativity$_3$). They are, moreover, symbol-systems without which we would be unable to understand creativity$_3$ itself and its coming into being. According to present evolutionary thinking, the symbolic order could not have come into existence without the 14 billion years of prior (non-symbolic) evolutionary development. There is no way, of course, for us to check this out apart from further symbolic testing and other imaginative activity (creativity$_3$). Although we have here a completely interdependent and coherent—and in that sense an intelligible—self-explanatory whole, it is a whole that in another sense remains completely inexplicable, a mystery.[18]

In our examination of the three modalities of creativity we have discovered that wherever we see—or come to believe—that creativity has occurred, we find mystery. This should not be difficult to understand: the modalities of creativity (as I have interpreted them) always involve the coming into being of something greater and more complex from something simpler and less complex. We humans ordinarily try to think of the coming into being of things in terms of ideas of cause and effect, but none of our conceptions of finite causality explain these kinds of development. And yet, our perception of and thinking about the world and ourselves within the world presents creative happenings of many sorts—whether we go back to the biblical account or focus on modern scientific ideas. I have suggested repeatedly in this book that it is not appropriate to reify creativity in any way, or to attribute it to some "being" (such as a creator conceived as an independent quasi-person); for it is precisely this developing *activity* (creativity) that should itself be thought of as God. This characterization of God as creativity is in a special way quite fitting, given the long history in the West that links all creativity with God (though God has usually not been thought of as "developing"). "Creativity" designates a referent for our God-talk that—although deeply mysterious—is specifiable in terms of today's understanding of the world and the human, and it does so without compromising the important traditional insistence that God must not be confused with any of the realities of the created order. God is *creativity*, not one of the creatures (though deeply involved with the creatures). Thinking of God in this way means (as we have seen) that God must be understood as ultimately mystery, beyond human comprehension.

Although God is not regarded here as a person and we are in no position to say what God *is*—God (in and through creativity$_3$) is clearly to be thought of as the ultimate source and ground of all our human realities, values, and meanings (including all Christian values and meanings). Thus, we *can* say something about how we are *related* to God, though what God (creativity) is remains a mystery. That we cannot know what God *is* but only how we are related to God has been a long-standing theological claim affirmed by such influential theologians as Maimonides, Thomas Aquinas, and Schleiermacher (see discussion of "negative theology" in the prologue, section V). And, as we have seen, the *mystery* of creativity—which I have been claiming throughout is what we should think of as God—is itself unqualified, is absolute. This not only rules out all anthropomorphism in our thinking of God (as I have frequently argued in this book), it has much more radical implications. The most basic claims about God in our

Western traditions—for example, that God is "being as such," God *necessarily* exists, or that God is *one* (being?) not many (monotheism)—are also put in question here. This does not mean these claims are false, that we should no longer accept them. What it does mean is that we are in no position to answer the question about their truth; what God (creativity) really *is* cannot be known by humans, it is beyond our cognitive reach. The radicality of this agnosticism would seem to dissolve away the question of whether it is appropriate to think of God (creativity) as "developing" or in other ways "changing," or whether we should try to think of God in terms of three (or more) creativities or only one that can be considered in three distinctly different contexts. This radicality means that when we are told to put our trust in the ultimate mystery of creativity, it is indeed a momentous act of faith that is being called for. It may be that our distress that such a radical agnosticism is required of us is actually grounded upon a long-standing Western assumption (going all the way back to Parmenides): the assumption that *being* must be regarded as the absolute foundation undergirding all life, reality, and thinking. If we had been brought up (as many Buddhists have) thinking in terms of *sunyata* (emptiness, nothingness) as ultimate, would we feel more at home with the radical faith that life now seems to require of us?[19]

From at least the time of Moses, God has been regarded as the source and ground of human morality, and for Christians that morality has been epitomized in the divine love (*agape*);[20] indeed, it was possible for the early Christians to go so far as to say flatly that "God is love" (1 John 4:8, 16). Can such claims as these be in any way accommodated to the idea of God as the creativity in and through which our vast (impersonal) universe has come into being, a creativity that often brings forth new realities through massive violent destruction of other realities already in place—exploding stars, cosmic "black holes" that swallow up everything in their vicinity; on planet Earth volcanic eruptions, earthquakes, floods, and so on, nature "red in tooth and claw"? This violence, it would seem, is deeply connected with the creativity manifest in the world, and if it suggests any kind of morality at all, many would say, it is a morality of naked power. Is not this sort of creativity, this sort of God-of-violent-power, at the antipodes of everything central to Christian faith?

As suggested in chapter 2, we do not need to draw that conclusion. We should see all of this as the creative beginnings and underpinnings of a remarkable trajectory in our universe that has eventuated in the creation of life and then much later in the creation of agents capable of self-conscious action and of making moral judgments about such matters as violence and nonviolence. The creativity (God) at work in our universe has brought us—in the course of our developing history—to a point where we can entertain the possibility of living in a moral order that is nonviolent, even loving, where we can deliberately choose (creativity$_3$) to work at bringing about such an order and can try to train ourselves and our children to live and act in nonviolent loving ways (however much we continue to fall short of actualizing such dreams). In the processes through which our humanness was created, activity, attitudes, and behavior of the sort we call *loving* emerged (creativity$_3$) and came into focus, and in our human corner of the universe capacities and needs for *agape*-love gradually became important and prized (at least in some quarters). So in and through the emergence of creativity$_3$ (our specifically human participation in creativity) loving, caring attitudes and activities—along with many other sorts—have become highly valued features of life. Nonviolent *agape*-love was created (during the biological evolution and historical development of life here on planet Earth) in the interplay of God (creativities$_{2,3}$) with emerging humankind. This development, quite unlike much of what apparently occurred in the interrelations of God with many other spheres of the cosmic order, is—at least in the judgment of those who count themselves as Christian—of great significance.[21]

God (creativity) has brought into being human persons and communities—in all their vast diversity—and God continues to sustain this great pluralism of human life.[22] This conception of God undercuts completely the anthropocentrism and anthropomorphism of the traditional Abrahamic understanding of God—and the consequent too-easy authorization of excessive violence and utterly inhuman forms of domination and warfare, as is so often found in the Abrahamic traditions. It presents us with an image/concept much better fitted to encourage our coming to terms with today's massive ecological and pluralistic issues—the central religious challenge of our time. [23] Obviously, however, it raises many new theological problems of its own.

There will be those who say that in this theology God has really disappeared in the mists of mystery and that true faith in God is thus also gone. To that I reply, true faith in God is not living with a conviction that everything is going to be okay in the end because we know that our heavenly father is taking care of us. It is, rather, acknowledging and accepting the ultimate mystery of things and, precisely in face of that mystery, going out like Abraham (as Hebrews 11:8 puts it) not really knowing where we are going, but nevertheless moving forward creatively and with confidence—confidence in the serendipitous creativity that has brought our trajectory and us into being, has continued to sustain the human project within the web of life that surrounds and nurtures us, and has given us a measure of hope for that project here on planet Earth. Since we now see that we are to love and give ourselves and our lives not only to our *human* neighbors and enemies, but also to the wider orders of life in which we find ourselves, this perspective deepens and widens the radicality of the Christian ethic, and thus the radicality of Christian faith.

• • •

In the beginning was creativity, and the creativity was with God, and the creativity was God. All things came into being through the mystery of creativity; apart from creativity nothing would have come into being.

The Development of My Theological Thinking: Two Themes

I am not a religious man but I cannot help seeing every problem from a religious point of view.

Ludwig Wittgenstein[1]

In this epilogue I take up two central themes with which I have been preoccupied throughout my life, and which are expressed in the development of my theological reflection from a very early age on: the problem of God—the questionableness of all our thinking and talking about God—and my life-long concern that human relations should be pervaded, above all, by loving, caring, responsible attitudes and activities. The more visible of these two themes in my writing has been my attempt to get clear, and to make new proposals respecting, the problematic character of God-talk today; but underlying, and deeply shaping my thinking about God (as I shall maintain in what follows), have been my moral commitments, my convictions about how we humans should live.[2]

I

I have no memory of a specific moment when the question of the intelligibility and plausibility of the central symbol of our Western religious traditions, "God," became an issue for me. But perplexity about what has been taken by Christians (and many others) to be the fundamental reality with which we humans have to do—a reality strongly affirmed in my home and childhood community—has been with me as far back as I can remember, sometimes becoming quite strong, sometimes receding, but always there. The "God is dead" theological movement of the 1960s sharply focused this question for me, and from that point on I felt increasingly driven to address it directly. It became clear to me in the mid-sixties that the so-called neoorthodox theology that had been dominant in this country among Protestants for several decades, and which I had more or less accepted in graduate school as the proper basis for my theological work, simply dodged the major issue of how God's reality was to be understood. It was necessary, therefore, to rethink from the ground up how theology was to be done. I began, thus, what was to become a fairly long period of reflection on questions of theological method: What is going on in theological work? With what sorts of themes does it deal? What kinds of claims can theologians properly make? What alternative methods and procedures are available to theologians? This culminated in the development of a conception of theology that I call *imaginative construction*, and in consequence I have been led to rethink the whole Christian theological enterprise from this standpoint. A central feature of this reconception is my proposal that the traditional metaphors of creator, lord, and father—on the basis of which the Western image/concept of God has been largely constructed—be replaced by the metaphor of *serendipitous creativity*, as we seek to construct a conception of God more appropriate to today's understandings of the world and of our human existence in it.

I grew up in a Mennonite home and community, and my second lifelong concern—that human relations should always be loving ones, even with those whom we take to be "enemies"—was a central Mennonite conviction. Going the second mile, turning the other cheek (Matt. 5:39-41), was strongly emphasized by my parents, and particularly well exemplified by my mother's demeanor and activities both at home and beyond; she was a much-loved person by all who knew her. It was a conviction also strongly emphasized in the community in which we lived, the campus of Bethel College, a Mennonite institution of which my father was president for many years. During my teens, in the 1940s, when America was preparing for and then actually became a participant in World War II, this community was a sanctuary for me and my pacifist convictions when patriotic fervor became strong in nearby Newton, Kansas, particularly in Newton High School. From an early age on, I have been convinced of the basic correctness of this Mennonite emphasis on how life should be lived;[3] and these Mennonite convictions underlie my attempts in recent years to sketch a Christian ethic in connection with my notion of humans as biohistorical beings, and to address theologically such knotty issues as the enormous religious and cultural pluralism of human existence, an issue with which we today must come to terms in a new way.

I was drafted as a conscientious objector in October of 1943, four months after I had turned eighteen, and was sent to Civilian Public Service Camp #5 in Colorado Springs, one of the camps administered by the Mennonite Central Committee. Later I was transferred to a state mental hospital in Ypsilanti, Michigan, and after that to Gulfport, Mississippi, where we made privies for poor people who had no sanitary facilities. During my year in Colorado Springs I read for the first time (with very little understanding) a book I would read many times over: Kant's *Critique of Pure Reason*. This and others of Kant's writings have influenced deeply my overall thinking on philosophical and theological issues; in particular, Kant has helped me to understand the bearing of the symbol "God" on the moral dimensions of human existence, and vice versa. I was also exploring religious questions in other less intellectual ways. I looked into studies of mysticism during these years, and writings by mystics. But, although mysticism has continued to interest me, this has always been from a distance, so to speak: I seem to be "tone deaf" with respect to so-called religious experience. When others speak of their "experience of God" or of "God's presence," or the profound experience of "the holy" or of "sacredness," I simply do not know what they are talking about. Perhaps this is one reason why the problem of God has been, throughout my life, so baffling and difficult. I have long since concluded that talk about *experience* of God involves what philosophers call a "category mistake," and should not, therefore, be engaged in. (My gradually developing understanding of the symbol "God" as a human imaginative construction [to be sketched in what follows] explains how and why I came to this conclusion.)[4]

After World War II, with my return to Bethel College to complete my bachelor's degree, it became clear that my earlier interest in the hard sciences was giving way to deep concerns about the meaning of human life and its proper ordering, and my academic work became increasingly concentrated in the social sciences and philosophy. At the time of my graduation in November 1947, my intention was to enter a doctoral program in philosophy, but before I did that I wanted (as I said to myself) to give the Christian faith "a last chance to say something to me" that I could take seriously. So I applied to Yale Divinity School for admission to the BD program (what we now call an MDiv degree), though I had no intention of going into the ministry.

The several months before that program was to begin were spent working toward a Master's degree in sociology at Northwestern University, studies that were to have a permanent impact on me. Three important developments should be mentioned. I became acquainted, for the first time, with the writings of George Herbert Mead and worked carefully through his posthumously published book, *Mind, Self, and Society* (1934). His claim that human selfhood and mentality were created in and developed to high levels through the evolution of language—and thus were thoroughly *social* in character—totally reversed the common-sense belief that language was the creation of mind with the contention that our human minds themselves were actually a product of increasingly complex linguisticality. This insight enabled Mead to give a convincing evolutionary account of the emergence of human mind on planet Earth, and also (by implication) an evolutionary account of human spirituality, including religion and morality. I found these ideas fascinating and persuasive. They expanded and deepened my interest in evolutionary theory and furthered my developing a naturalistic understanding of everything human.

Second, during these months at Northwestern (I'm not sure just when or how) I became acquainted with Ludwig Feuerbach's mid-nineteenth-century book, *The Essence of Christianity* ([1841] 1957), which argued that what had hitherto been thought of as *theology* was really disguised *anthropology* (human studies). Feuerbach showed that all the major doctrines of Christian faith—including especially the doctrine of God—could be understood as expressions of an unconscious projection of human characteristics and qualities onto a nonexistent external cosmic reality; specifically theological claims, thus, should also be understood naturalistically.

Third, during the summer term at Northwestern I was permitted to join a special graduate seminar, conducted jointly by the chairpersons of the departments of sociology, psychology, and anthropology. We took up exciting interdisciplinary problems, and I presented a paper posing questions about the psychological, social, and cultural relativism that everyone in the seminar (including me) seemed to take for granted. My interest in this problem had perhaps begun with my experience as a conscientious objector, when I tried to understand why the Mennonite "cognitive minority" of which I was a member, and the much larger majority of American Christians, disagreed so completely about the rightness and wrongness of participation in the killing of war—each side being thoroughly convinced it knew what was truly right. These questions deepened at Ypsilanti State Hospital when I encountered delusional patients who took themselves to be living in entirely different worlds from the one that I, and most others about me, took for granted. How could this drastic difference in our most basic judgments of reality, truth, and right be understood? Is everyone living in his or her own private delusional world, from which there is no possible escape? Are all human judgments relative to the psychological, social, and cultural contexts within which they are made? But wouldn't such a conclusion undermine the possibility of making any truly valid judgments about anything?

These are the issues I presented to the seminar, finishing up with one last question: If we take the concept of psychological, social, and cultural relativism seriously, must we not draw the conclusion that this very concept—which all of us in the seminar took for granted—is itself in question? Imagine my surprise and disappointment when no one agreed with me on the importance of this problem: in this seminar, I was told, we were dealing with psychological, social, and cultural *facts*—not with confusing philosophical questions and theories. If I wished to pursue these obscure and probably insoluble issues, I would have to go to some other department of the university. I received my MA in sociology from Northwestern at the end of the summer, and by that time it had become clear that to deal with the questions in which I was most interested, I would have to go to "some other department." I was ready to take my concerns and problems to Divinity School.

II

The Yale Divinity School that I entered in 1948 at age twenty-three was dominated by a basically neoorthodox theology with a strong social ethics component and was thus equipped nicely to assist me in thinking through the two central themes in which I was particularly interested. Professor H. Richard Niebuhr was working out a way of reconciling a thoroughgoing conception of human historicity (including historical relativism) with Christian faith and its claims about divine revelation.[5] Moreover, in doing this he drew upon and amplified G. H. Mead's social theory of human selfhood and mind, and (in some of his seminars and lectures) took up figures like Feuerbach and showed how they too could be fitted into—indeed, could make a significant contribution to—his sociohistorical conception of human life and Christian faith. All of this was quite appealing to me.

Niebuhr argued that all humans were to be understood as significantly shaped by the historical and communal context within which they emerged and were gradually formed into responsible selves; for most of their lives people inevitably live and work largely in terms of such communally-shaped values and meanings. This explained well my own experience and self-understanding. It fitted into Mennonite emphases on the importance of taking seriously Mennonite community meanings and values, and it helped me understand why others, growing up within and informed by quite different communal values and meanings, disagreed so decisively with us Mennonites. Moreover, with this understanding it was possible to think of God not so much as an extremely problematic and uncertain mysterious something-or-other—the reality and significance of which had to be established before faith could be possible—but rather as a central meaning and value orienting Christian faith and life. "God" was seen as the principal focusing symbol in the Christian way of understanding life and the world.

The question of God, thus, was to be addressed in terms of whether one wanted to live a Christian life, not in terms of some abstract notion of truth. In this way my two lifelong themes began to come together and reinforce each other. Life is oriented with reference to God when it is ordered in Christian terms. What is *morally required* in human living, not some supposedly autonomous epistemological norms, is the pertinent issue here. One's moral stance—including the set of meanings and values, symbols and rituals, in terms of which one's life is oriented and formed—is the basic ground for faith in God. (This was obviously a strongly Kantian move in Niebuhr, and also increasingly in me.) Although my convictions about the validity of a radical Mennonite Christian ethic were somewhat threatened by the essentially Calvinist social ethics of Niebuhr, Liston Pope, and others at Yale Divinity School, they were not destroyed but rather became better nuanced through these reflections; thus (especially in the context of conversations with some of the other pacifists there, of which there were very few in the student body) they were in fact deepened.

These developments led me to consider taking my doctorate in theology instead of philosophy, as I had been planning. Upon inquiry, I discovered that if I entered Yale's doctoral program in philosophy, I would not be permitted to continue theological studies to the extent I wished, but that if I enrolled in the Divinity School's program in philosophical theology, I could take as many philosophy courses as I liked. So I decided to stay in the Divinity School. (I had already been taking numerous courses in philosophy during my BD studies, and I continued that when I entered the doctoral program in theology.) My growing convictions about the interconnections of theology and ethics also led me to seek ordination as a Mennonite minister, when I left Yale in 1953 to take a position in the Department of Religion at Pomona College (Claremont, California). Though I did not intend to become a church pastor, my Mennonite connections and stance were important to me, and I wanted to speak and write as an authorized interpreter of a Mennonite understanding of Christian faith and life. I was ordained in my home church on the Bethel campus.

At Pomona College my teaching was lodged substantially in two large introductory courses in Bible, one in Old Testament, the other in New Testament. I also taught courses in philosophy of religion and ethics. Any courses in theology proper, however, were ruled out by my department chairman as probably unacceptable to the rest of the faculty and certainly impolitic to propose. At this time I became increasingly interested in the writings of Karl Barth, including his commentary on Paul's letter to the Romans, which seemed to illuminate in a striking way my own faith-situation. Barth presented a highly dialectical conception of faith: as our principal human connection with God, faith must be seen—following Paul, Augustine, Luther, and others—as God's gift. Humans can in no way bring themselves into a stance of faith by their own efforts, however sincere and persistent. Thus, the more we try to believe in God, and the more we believe that such efforts are warranted, the farther we are from true faith. And, paradoxically, the more we recognize our unfaith, our doubts, our disobedience—and thus freely acknowledge our alienation from God, our sinfulness—the more we actually stand before God in faith. So precisely my deep, troubling doubts and disbelief, with which I had been preoccupied for years, could be seen as actually marks of faith in God? Very puzzling, and very paradoxical, but that seemed to be the conclusion to be drawn from Barth's highly dialectical and rhetorically powerful analysis. This is what the Protestant doctrine of justification by grace through faith was all about. With the help of H. R. Niebuhr and Karl Barth—and also Paul Tillich (a figure taken up in my dissertation) who had actually developed a notion of "justification by *doubt*"—I was finding my way into a theological stance within which I could live productively and fruitfully.

This dialectical approach helped me to develop further my thinking on the problem of relativism, since it left me completely free theologically to work out a thoroughly this-worldly, and thus naturalistic and historicistic, understanding of the relativities of human life and the human pursuit of truth. My doctoral dissertation was on "The Problem of Relativism and the Possibility of Metaphysics" (Kaufman 1955). With the help of writings by Paul Tillich, R. G. Collingwood, and Wilhelm Dilthey, I worked through an extensive study of the literature on relativism and historicity and developed a constructive position of my own on these matters. The dissertation proposed an understanding of human existence and knowledge as always actively responding to demands of the living existential *present*, a present inexorably shaped by a particular historical past but ineluctably moving forward in anticipation of a relatively open and unknown future. So we live and work and think, as best we can, in the present in which we find ourselves—never, of course, escaping the relativities of that present—as we seek to resolve the problems that confront us in our movement into the future. My dissertation was completed in the spring of 1955, and in 1960 a revised version was published under the title of *Relativism, Knowledge, and Faith*, my first book. In my dissertation and this book are to be found seeds of much of my later thinking about epistemological, anthropological, and theological issues.

I left Pomona College in 1958 to join the faculty of Vanderbilt Divinity School as Associate Professor of Theology. There, for the first time, I had to put together a yearlong set of lectures on systematic theology. So I worked out conceptions of creation, the fall, and sin; the doctrine of the trinity and christology; evil and eschatology; Christian ethics and the moral life; theological method; and so on. (In all of this, I was beginning to discover the extent to which Christian theology must be understood as basically human imaginative construction!) In 1959 I was invited to give the Menno Simons Lectures at Bethel College, and I took that opportunity to sketch in five lectures the overall theological position I was developing. It was a theology grounded essentially on the moral necessities of human life, presenting the central Christian claims about God and Christ, humanity and the world, as a kind of picture of human existence and its context that served well and made intelligible our human moral responsibilities and decision-making. These lectures, revised and somewhat enlarged, were the basis of a small book published in 1961 as *The Context of Decision*.

The systematic theology that I was working out at Vanderbilt was thoroughly historicist in character. Following H. R. Niebuhr, I argued that we humans always live out of the symbol-system that we have inherited, and that Christians, therefore, need make no apologies for, nor attempt to justify, their attention to and concern about the central symbols that give form to their faith, their living, their thinking (an assumption I would soon put sharply into question). The problematic dimensions of Christian God-talk were handled simply by saying (confessionally): this is the world-picture with which we Christians live and work; this is the way we organize our lives and thinking; we recognize, of course, that there are many other symbolic pictures by means of which humans orient their lives, and this is ours. My experience as a conscientious objector in World War II had taught me that even though we may regard our way of living and thinking as right and true, we must be willing to live with and in the midst of other quite different ways of ordering life, as we seek to love our neighbors (Christians and others) as ourselves—even though we believe these others are completely wrong in many of their ideas and attitudes.

Here my moral concerns about how we ought to live were clearly beginning to outrank and to reshape my thinking about human truth-claims, so often regarded as absolute and not to be compromised. It was a kind of Christian *pluralism* that I was working toward here (though that word was not available to me at that time) and this later served as the model for my reflection on problems of religious and cultural pluralism generally, and for my development of the notion of pluralistic or dialogical truth as a way of moving beyond the impasse created by the diverse truth-claims emphasized in different religious traditions.[6] But none of this was clearly visible at that time. My *ethical* convictions (basically still Mennonite) were for me more important and more certain than any others, and this meant I already had in place a standpoint that implied we should deal tolerantly with the variety of human faith-stances, not only among Christians but in the wider world as well. Humanly more important, and thus more fundamental, than any truth questions—about which there would always be doubts and other problems, never certainty—is the moral question of how we humans are to live together in the world in which we find ourselves. In my theology lectures at Vanderbilt, in my Menno Simons lectures, and in some other writings for Mennonite publications, I worked out my earliest formulations of these issues.

When I finally published my *Systematic Theology: A Historicist Perspective* in 1968 all these matters, and many others, had been pulled together into a systematic statement of what I took to be the major Christian contentions and concepts, inherited from nearly two thousand years of history, that were still plausible. To make such a contemporary, comprehensive, fresh reinterpretation of the received Christian symbol-system, in all its finely-wrought details, was what, during those early years of teaching, I understood systematic theology to be all about. Though in these views I was taking up the essentially confessional neoorthodox stance that I had acquired at Yale Divinity

School, there were some harbingers of things to come. Here are some examples: In the preface, the book was characterized as "a work of the theological imagination" (xv), not simply as a new interpretation of tradition, an idea I was later to develop into a full-blown revisionary conception of theological method. The entirety of chapter 28, deliberately avoiding the tendency of many theologians to tip-toe around sensitive issues, was devoted to a thorough discussion of Jesus' alleged resurrection in which the conclusion was reached that it was not plausible today to hold that the historical Jesus had come back to life again after his crucifixion; this implied, moreover, that Christian hope should no longer be understood as involving life after death for us mortals (464–71). In chapter 19, a theological outline of "The History of the World," contemporary astrophysical, biological, and historical thinking was employed in a sketch of cosmic and human development from the origins of the universe (as then understood) to the present, clearly anticipating what is now worked out in the present volume. All of this, however, was laid out in the largely confessional terms that I had appropriated from H. R. Niebuhr and Karl Barth.

This approach to theology, however—though it reconciled in certain respects the two basic themes that had been driving my intellectual activities—was proving increasingly unsatisfactory to me. Partly because of my growing sense of the artificiality of Barth's highly dialectical interpretation of faith, which had enabled me to put aside for awhile the doubts and unbelief in which I found myself; partly due to the impact of the so-called Death of God discussions among theologians in the early 1960s, in which I was participating, I began to move away from this neoorthodox confessionalism. In my last years at Vanderbilt and my early years at Harvard (where I moved in 1963), I increasingly came to see that *God* was the principal theme—and also a major *problem*—with which Christian theology had to come to terms, and the largely confessional approach I had been following simply ignored the problematic dimensions of our God-talk.

III

I sought to formulate and address the issues I was beginning to discern in a number of essays, some of them initially published before my *Systematic Theology* came into print. And during our family's second sabbatical leave in 1969–70 at Oxford (the first had been in Tübingen, Germany, in 1961–62) it became increasingly clear that I was now moving to a quite different standpoint. My new way of thinking began to show itself especially in a lecture entitled "God as Symbol." This was written in England and presented there several times, and an expanded version of it was published in 1972 as chapter 5 of my next book, *God the Problem* (1972a). In that book, in addition to the contention that we order our lives largely in terms of certain fundamental *symbols*, and that it is the business of theology to examine, analyze, and assess these symbols and symbol-systems, it was stated forthrightly that the only possible test of our central symbols is pragmatic:

> There is no way to establish the "truth" of the notion of God by ordinary rational or philosophical argument: that is in principle impossible. The only relevant question of truth . . . here concerns that ordering of life and the world which faith imposes: is such an ordering of the world appropriate to the world as we experience it and to the nature of our human existence, or does it involve misapprehensions of our situation and result in a stunting of human life and its ultimate breakdown? Is some other fundamental paradigm or "root metaphor" more apposite or adequate for grasping the world so as to enhance and deepen human life, or does the theistic imagery and pattern most effectively perform this function? (99)

Note that in this passage a major criterion for assessing theological truth-claims—a *pragmatic* criterion—is *the way the symbol "God" enables us to live in the world*.

As I was writing that lecture and essay, it became clear to me that I was now working within a quite different way of thinking about the theological enterprise: theology was really to be understood as through-and-through *human imaginative construction* of a world-picture that could orient human life;[7] a theological picture was distinguished from other similar imaginative constructions, not by its grounding in divine revelation as the neoorthodox and much of the theological tradition as a whole had held, but rather in its utilization of the master-symbol *God* to bring all dimensions of its world-picture into focus. All claims about divine revelation were part of our God-talk, and were thus *derivative* from what was implied by the symbol "God." Since the notion of revelation itself thus presupposed, and indeed employed, the symbol "God," it could not properly be regarded as the principal ground justifying our human use of this word. This meant that some new questions needed to be addressed by theologians, questions of this sort: How and why did this particular symbol ("God") come to be deployed by (some) humans in their world-pictures? Out of what materials has the human imagination constructed this symbol? How is it held before the mind—in prayer and worship? in contemplation? in day-to-day life? in theological reflection? Does it perform certain unique functions for humans? Are there some distinctive dangers to human life and well-being to which the employment of this symbol may give rise, or which it may aggravate? And so on. In the last days of our stay in Oxford, I hastily wrote a paper (largely for myself) entitled simply "Theology as Construction," in which I attempted to sketch in broad strokes the conception of theology now beginning to come into view. This paper was the first draft of the central chapter in my next small book (published in 1975), to be called *An Essay on Theological Method* (Kaufman 1995).[8]

Theology is here acknowledged as through-and-through *human* work, a constructive activity of the imagination (as Feuerbach had argued). If we are to engage in this work self-consciously and deliberately, along what lines should our constructive activity proceed? What objectives should we set for ourselves? In terms of what norms should we judge our work? How can we do this work of imaginative construction most effectively? Directly implied in this understanding, of course, was that theology is no longer to be thought of as basically a hermeneutical task, simply interpreting God's revelation in the Bible and tradition for a new day. So methodological issues now became a high priority on my theological agenda. *An Essay on Theological Method* was my first attempt to address these issues in print and, in its latest revised edition (1995), it remains my clearest and most compact statement on them (along with a short piece most recently revised and republished under the title, "Theology: Critical, Constructive, and Contextualized" in Kaufman 1996a, chapter 2).

I shall not summarize the argument of the *Essay* here, but I will note briefly what is taken up in its three main chapters. Chapter 1 argues that (as I just suggested) *God* is the central theme that distinguishes theology from other intellectual endeavors, and this theme is highly problematic. A brief sketch is presented of the way the word "God" is used in English-language discourse, and some of the peculiarities of this word and its usage are laid out. (The influence of Ludwig Wittgenstein and other "ordinary language" philosophers was making itself evident here). The second chapter argues that all speaking and thinking of God, even of the most simple and unsophisticated sort—our prayers to God, our worship of God, our reflection on God—*presupposes* constructive imaginative activity and would be impossible without it. The task of formal theology now becomes one of developing norms for judging the effectiveness and validity with which this imaginative work has been carried out in the past and proposing criteria that will help us assess our own attempts to carry through this constructive work today. The third chapter brings the book to a conclusion in its argument that there are three indispensable constituents of all adequate theological thinking. The first is "the explicit development of a conception of the overall context within which [our human] experience falls, a concept of the world" (56). The second is construction of a "concept of God, of that further reality which relativizes and limits the world and all that is in it," including, of course, humans (59). The third is reformulation of the concept of world so that it "fits" intelligibly with "the God thought to be its ultimate ground and limit"; that is, the third is careful adjustment of "each of these [two] concepts to the other" so that "a theistic interpretation or understanding of the world . . . [is] developed" along with a viable conception of God (71). It is claimed that if these several tasks are not all carried through carefully, theological work will be faulty and inadequately presented and argued. This methodological stance has governed all my subsequent theological work.[9] (It may be remarked that the "three indispensable constituents of . . . adequate theological thinking" mentioned here are central to the argument of this present book.)

The *Essay* is, of course, only a methodological sketch. It was first published just a year before my wife, Dorothy, our youngest child, and I, were to go to Bangalore, India, where I would teach in the United Theological College for two terms, testing out some of my ideas for the first time in a non-Western setting. This was an important year for all of us, enabling us to get some distance on the Western culture and forms of life that we had largely taken for granted. In my *Essay on Theological Method* I had been careful to note from time to time that what I was proposing was all expressed in terms of *Western* theological and philosophical concepts, methods, languages, and traditions, and that I could not, therefore, make universalistic claims for it. It was very gratifying, however, to discover rather quickly that this way of thinking freed my Indian students to do their theologizing in terms directly pertinent to their own religious and cultural context, instead of confining themselves to repeating the rigid propositions of the Euro-American theology handed down to them and regarded as universally normative by missionaries and their disciples. This involved, of course, a relativizing of theological truth-claims in light of what was *morally demanded* for ongoing human living in the Indian socio-historical context. My experience in India brought me into direct contact with many different religions and cultures, and I began to see that all these fascinating forms of symbolization, ritual, and morality—these exceedingly diverse ways of thinking about the world and human existence in it, and of attempting to live fruitfully within the order and orientation provided by these various inherited symbol-systems—were also to be understood as products of human imaginative creativity adapting itself in diverse locations to a wide range of historical and geographical settings and circumstances.

This experience encouraged me to attempt to construct a Christian theology open to and appreciative of the many different cultures and religions around the world, and while in India I began to sketch for myself outlines and notes for developing such a theology. But it would take fifteen years and more to give it satisfactory form. In those intervening years Dorothy and I would make a number of visits to Japan, visits to South Africa, Israel, and China, another visit to India, and several to England, and I became regularly engaged in Buddhist-Christian dialogue both in Japan and the United States, and more briefly in Jewish-Muslim-Christian dialogue in the Near East and in the United States. I attempted to take into account these broadening and deepening experiences as I gradually worked away in class lectures and in essays on what would finally be published in 1993 as *In Face of Mystery: a Constructive Theology* (Kaufman 1993a).[10] During this period I found myself gradually giving up the personalistic side of the traditional Christian conception of God—which until then had been at the center of my theological reflection—as I attempted to appropriate new cosmological and ecological thinking. An adequate contemporary constructive theology (it seemed to me) must take into account what we have learned about the evolutionary character of our world and ourselves in the modern astrophysical, geological, biological, ecological, social, and historical sciences. (Chapters 1 to 3 in this book present some of this thinking). In the *Essay on Theological Method* I had already suggested that an "existentialist" constructive theology (as I entitled it at that time), though it has a certain plausibility and some seeming advantages over the "cosmological" approach I was pursuing, was not really adequate today (see Kaufman 1995, chapter 3, notes 8 and 18).

The first clear sign that I was getting seriously concerned about the basic anthropomorphism and anthropocentrism of traditional

Christian thinking about God had appeared before the *Essay on Theological Method* was written: it is to be found in a paper, "A Problem for Theology: The Concept of Nature," prepared for the American Theological Society meeting in the spring of 1972.[11] In it I argued that there is a fundamental tension—indeed, a conceptual and logical incompatibility—between, on the one hand, the traditional personalistic understanding of God, and of God's intimate relation to humanity, and on the other hand, our growing awareness that human existence is essentially constituted by, and could not exist apart from, the complex ecological ordering of life that has evolved on planet Earth over many millennia. At that time, however, I could see no way of overcoming this incompatibility of naturalistic and theistic ways of thinking. It was only in consequence of my new methodological approach—and further reflection on these questions over the next twenty years—that, with *In Face of Mystery*, I finally found my way through this impasse.

My explicit movement away from traditional Christian thinking of God as a personal being first appeared publicly (I think) in my presidential address on "Nuclear Eschatology and the Study of Religion" before the American Academy of Religion in 1982.[12] I argued there (and more fully later on in Kaufman 1985) that the notion of God's providential care was getting in the way of our taking seriously our full human responsibility for the nuclear crisis in the midst of which we were living:

> Christian theologians and ordinary Christian believers alike . . .
> dare no longer simply assume that we know from authoritative tradition or past revelation the correct values and standards, i.e., the correct faith-orientation, in terms of which life is to be understood and decisions and actions are to be formulated. . . . [We] must be prepared to enter into the most radical kind of deconstruction and reconstruction of the traditions [we] have inherited, including especially the most central and precious symbols of these traditions, *God* and *Jesus Christ*.

In the little book, *Theology for a Nuclear Age*, based on my Ferguson Lectures at the University of Manchester (in England) and soon to follow my Academy address, I suggested briefly the kind of reconstruction of the image/concept of God that I had in mind: we should replace the anthropomorphic notion of God, as a kind of cosmic person/agent, with the much vaguer idea of the *"hidden creativity* at work in the historico-cultural process [and in] . . . the complex of physical, biological, and historico-cultural conditions which have made human existence possible, which continue to sustain it, and which draw it out to a fuller humanity and humaneness" (Kaufman 1985, 41–42; emphasis added).[13] These ideas were worked out in some detail in the constructive theology later published as *In Face of Mystery* (1993a).

IV

I cannot summarize that large book here,[14] but that is not necessary since the present volume is devoted to clarification and extension of some of the major ideas set forth there; and chapters 1 and 2 are occupied largely with these matters (see especially chapter 1 for summary statements of three of the key concepts developed in *In Face of Mystery*: humans as *biohistorical* beings and God conceived as the *serendipitous creativity* manifest in many different *trajectories* throughout the universe). The perspective developed in connection with these concepts has important implications for the way we think about ethics. The Christian ethic that we have inherited was focused almost entirely on our attitudes toward, and interactions with, other persons or personal beings. But if God is understood now as the creativity manifest throughout the cosmos, and we humans are understood as deeply embedded in, and basically sustained by, the web of life on planet Earth, then our attitudes and activities are to be ordered in terms of (a) what fits properly into this web of living creativity, all members of which are neighbors that we should love, and (b) what is in response to, and further contributes to, the ongoing creative development of our trajectory (the activity of God) within this web. Thus, the two central themes of my life and my theological reflection—the problematic of faith in God and the deep conviction about the significance of radical Christian ethics—meld into a unified naturalistic/historicistic conception of human existence in a world pervaded by serendipitous creativity.

As I have reflected in recent years on Nietzsche's cry that "God is dead," and reassessed it from the standpoint of my proposal that we think of God as creativity—keeping in mind that Nietzsche (as much as I) strongly emphasizes creativity—I have come to see (more clearly than earlier in my life) that for me as for Nietzsche the traditional anthropomorphic God has long since died. It was precisely the authority (and authoritarianism) of that God with which I was struggling for much of my life, and which (for a long time) I found difficult to repudiate. But with my realization that theology is, and always has been, essentially an activity of human imaginative construction, I came to understand this development as the death of a particular human symbolic formation—a symbolism doubtless very important in Western religions and thus in Western history (and in my own life), but one that is no longer pertinent to or nourishing of our human condition today. Theologians should not, however, give up their vocation to think through the problematics of our God-talk and our faith in God—that would be to throw out the baby with the bath. They are called, rather, to seek to reimagine, reconceive, reconstruct the symbol "God" with metaphors drawn from the ways in which we now understand ourselves and our world. This is, of course, precisely what I am attempting to do in this volume.

For traditional Mennonite understandings of Christian faith, what was most important for humans was not the creeds that we confess but how we live our lives in the midst of our neighbors and our enemies: we should be concerned about all our fellow humans and seek to live among them in love and in service to their needs. In continuing to hold this conviction (now in an ecologically expanded form) I remain, of course, very distant from Nietzsche, who focused his life and hopes on the glorious creativity of the *Übermensch*, show-ing little concern for all those "little men" roundabout whom he scorned. In my view, only as we give our lives in service (as Matt. 25:40 put it) to "the least of these" little men and women on Earth, and to the processes that sustain all of Earth's creatures, do we gain true human dignity and fulfillment. Not because an authoritarian divine king has so ordered things, but simply (and this is one of the mysteri-ous serendipities of history) because the supposed divine authority of that king, and of a man thought to be his "only begotten son," led to the formation of historical traditions that emphasized the radical ethic of *agape*-love, of forgiveness and reconciliation, as the right way to live humanly and humanely—a way appropriate even, perhaps especially, now (as we today are in a position to see) in this our ecologically-ordered cosmos, pervaded as it is by glorious creativity.

Preface

1. These developments in my thinking are sketched more fully in the autobiographical epilogue of this book; see especially pp. 119–26.

2. I want to thank the following persons for their indispensable help: Philip Clayton, Francis Fiorenza, James Gustafson, Van Harvey, Kimerer LaMothe, Jerry Regier, Mark C. Taylor, and Maurice Wiles.

Prologue

1. Our colleague, David Lamberth, provided us with this quotation.

Chapter 1

1. In this chapter a simplified conception of the *theological structure* of Christian faith is presented. For a more adequate discussion of this matter see Kaufman 1993a, especially chapters 6 and 7, in which a four-fold "categorial structure" of Christian faith is outlined. In parts II–IV of that book this outline is filled in, greatly complexified, and ultimately transformed when a trinitarian conception of God is developed.

129

2. In much of the rest of this chapter, I have lifted language from my article, "Ecological Consciousness and the Symbol 'God'" (Kaufman 2000).

3. This complicated development will be further explored in chapter 3 (see especially sections II–IV).

4. A great deal more, of course, needs to be said about the three concepts I am introducing here. For extended discussion see Kaufman 1993a; for my most recent reflection on serendipitous creativity, see chapters 2 and 3 below.

5. In the epilogue of this book I sketch more fully the connections of a christocentric theism with the overall theological program proposed here. See also Kaufman 1993a, chapters 25 to 27 and Kaufman 1996a, especially chapters 7 and 9. In these latter two books I sketch a "wider christology" not exclusively focused on the man Jesus.

Chapter 2

1. In many current discussions of religion and science issues by theologians, who otherwise seek to take modern evolutionary biology and cosmology seriously, there is a failure to come to terms directly with the problem stated here. See, for example, John Polkinghorne's subtle consideration of the idea of God's action in the world, in his otherwise excellent article "Chaos Theory and Divine Action": "The picture is . . . of an open future in which both human and divine agency play parts in its accomplishment. Christian theology has, at its best, striven to find a way between two unacceptably extreme pictures of God's relationship to the creation. One is that of the Cosmic Tyrant, who brings everything about by divine will alone. Such a God is the puppet master of the universe. . . . The detached God of deism, who simply watches it all happen, is another extreme, unacceptable to Christian thought. We seek a middle way in which God interacts with the creation without over-ruling it. . . . All that we are attempting to do in the present discussion is to show that one can take with all seriousness all that science tells us about the workings of the world, and still believe in a God who has not left the divine nature so impotent

that providence cannot act continuously and consistently with cosmic history" (1996, 249). In this article Polkinghorne takes "with all seriousness all that science tells us about the workings of the world" with the exception of a *central* scientific understanding: that complex features found in our world, such as conscious intention, purposive action, deliberate creation of artifacts, loving attitudes and behaviors, and the like, can come into being only *after* billions of years of complex cosmic, biological, and historical development have provided the necessary conditions for their emergence to occur. But in the anthropomorphic model in terms of which Polkinghorne's God is conceived, these sorts of features are all taken for granted as present and active through all eternity. So Polkinghorne simply ignores an important scientific contention about complex realities, a rather important exception to his claim to take "with all seriousness" what science tells us about these sorts of things. Further discussion of these matters will be found in chapter 3, especially sections I and III.

2. As brain scientist Terrence Deacon has observed: "Evolution is the one kind of process able to produce something out of nothing. . . . [A]n evolutionary process is an origination process. . . . Evolution is the author of its spontaneous creations" (1997, 458).

3. A full discussion of these pros and cons can be found in my book, Kaufman 1993a (see especially chapters 19 to 22).

4. For elaboration, see the discussion of the "serendipity of history" in Kaufman 1993a, 273–80.

5. In recent theorizing about *complexity*, as it develops in highly intricate networks of life (and elsewhere), it is argued that changes may reach an unforeseeable "tipping point" where previous organizational patterns break down and new ones begin to emerge, thus bringing into being novel forms. For discussion of this sort of ongoing creativity in the world, see chapter 3, section III.

6. I do not discuss the Big Bang in this chapter, but it is taken up in some detail in chapter 3. It is worth noting here, however, that it does not answer the question of why there is something, not nothing. We have no way of thinking of a purely spontaneous event because in

all our experience events occur in a context in which they are preceded, surrounded, and followed by other events, so the very concept of "event" precludes the idea of any sort of absolute beginning. Augustine long ago was aware of these problems. Modern cosmologists are also aware of them, and are attempting to think of ways to contextualize the Big Bang. For discussions of these issues, see chapter 3, section I.

7. Quoted by R. Otto in *The Idea of the Holy* ([1917] 1950, 25).

8. This sort of move—enhancing the mystery-dimension of our God-talk by focusing on the metaphor of creativity, thus ceasing to reify person-agent metaphors—has the further advantage of facilitating conversation between Christian theologians and adherents to certain of the reflective dimensions of East Asian cultures. The Buddhist metaphor of *sunyata* (emptiness, nothingness), for example, seems to carry some motifs similar to the idea of creativity. Confucian thinking about "Heaven" and Taoist ideas of chaos also manifest similarities. Replacing the reifying notion of God as creator with creativity, in our theological reflection, may help prepare for more fruitful conversations with, and even collaborative thinking with, representatives of these East Asian traditions.

9. This linkage between *God* and the *coming into being of the new in time* was made long ago by Isaiah, who portrays Yahweh as saying: "I am about to do a new thing: now it springs forth, do you not perceive it? . . . From this time forward I make you hear new things, hidden things that you have not known. They are created now, not long ago; before today you have never heard of them, so that you could not say, 'I already knew them'" (43:19; 48:6-8). For further discussion, see chapter 3.

10. For a summary of the details of the very close margins that have made these developments in cosmic evolution possible, see Rees 1997, chapter 14. See also William J. Broad, "Maybe We Are Alone in the Universe, After All" (2000). Some further discussion of these matters will be found in chapter 3 of this book, section III. If one takes claims such as these "with all seriousness" (as Polkinghorne puts it [see note 1]) how is it possible to continue to think of God as

a human-like person/agent existing before and independent of any such complex developments?

11. It is important to recognize that the notion of serendipitous creativity accomplishes this objective without leading into or providing grounds for a teleological argument for the existence of (an agential) God. This is, thus, a modest or "weak" anthropism. See Rees 1997, chapter 15, for a thoughtful, brief discussion of various sorts of anthropic thinking. For an early full discussion of "the anthropic principle," see John D. Barrow and Frank J. Tipler's book, *The Anthropic Cosmological Principle* (1988).

12. I characterize a faith-stance as "radically christomorphic" if it takes such New Testament emphases as (a) Jesus' radical teaching to "love your enemies" (Matt. 5:43-48), (b) the nonresistant posture of Jesus himself in facing his own enemies and acceding to his crucifixion, and (c) the Pauline admonition to have "the same mind be in you that was in Christ Jesus, [who having] emptied himself, taking the form of a slave, ... humbled himself and became obedient to the point of death—even death on a cross" (Phil. 2:5, 7-8), to be paradigmatic for understanding what it means to regard God as "love" (1 John 4) and for defining the radical stance that is (should be) normative for Christian life and action. For elaboration, see Kaufman 1993a, chapters 25 and 26.

13. For further discussion of this issue, see my article "Is God Nonviolent?" (Kaufman 2003).

14. For fuller discussion of our human biohistorical reality, and the biohistorical trajectory that has brought us into being, see chapter 1, section II of this book, and especially chapter 3, sections II–IV; see also Kaufman 1993a, parts II and III.

15. A discussion of issues related to this will be found in chapter 3, section IV.

16. For further discussion of these issues, see Kaufman 1993a, especially chapter 24. See also Baruch Spinoza, *Ethics*, part IV (Spinoza [1677] 1989).

17. For further discussion of the problem of evil, see Kaufman 1993a, especially chapters 15 and 24.

18. This was also a note in traditional Christian thinking: "Work out your own salvation with fear and trembling; for it is God [i.e. creativity] who is at work in you, enabling you both to will and to work" (Phil. 2: 12).

Chapter 3

1. "A mystery is something we find we cannot think clearly about, cannot get our minds around, cannot manage to grasp. . . . We are indicating that what we are dealing with here seems to be beyond what our minds can handle. . . . 'Mystery' is . . . a grammatical or linguistic operator by means of which we remind ourselves of something about ourselves: that at this point we are using our language in an unusual, limited, and potentially misleading way" (Kaufman 1993a, 60-61).

2. We are inclined to take it for granted that we understand the meaning of the word "billions" here because it has a clearly defined place in our number system, but this is really a very abstract kind of understanding. Numbers of this size are completely beyond imagination—that is, no appropriate *image* of them can be produced by our minds—though they can be conceived abstractly; i.e. we can *think* them. Consider, for example, the impossibility of distinguishing the "image" of one billion grains of sand from the image of 990 million grains. (For a popular discussion of these matters, see Denison 2002.) Considerations like these further deepen the profound mystery in what we are discussing here, and we need to remember this when we are told about "billions" of this and "billions" of that—as will frequently occur in what follows.

3. For theological elaboration of this notion of God as serendipitous creativity, see Kaufman 1993a, chapters 19 to 27. For later refinements of this notion, see chapter 2 of this book.

4. See, for example, philosopher Loyal Rue: "Instead of fragmenting into subdisciplines, the sciences are now merging into cross disciplines. The most exciting theoretical advances in science in recent decades are the ones that have managed to integrate the sciences of

the large with the sciences of the small. In physics, . . . astronomy has been theoretically coupled with particle physics to produce quantum cosmology. In biology, evolutionary theory has been coupled with molecular biology to produce the grand synthesis. In psychology, neurology has been coupled with cognitive theory and other disciplines to produce the integrated cognitive sciences. . . . Especially important are the links between biology and the physical sciences on the one side, and between biology and the social sciences on the other. . . . Today the paradigm of evolution is rapidly becoming the organizing principle for all the sciences—the physical sciences, the life sciences, and the social sciences. . . . The unifying insight behind this integration of the sciences is that the entire universe is evolving. The universe is a single reality . . . of interconnected events. The universe is not a place where evolution happens, *it is* the evolution happening." (2000, 42-43).

5. A recent article by Dennis Overbye (2002) sums up the various dimensions of this emerging consensus.

6. Not everyone agrees with Hawking on this point. For a different view, see Rees 1997.

7. In what is largely a later version of his book, Hawking modifies this slightly, no longer declaring the irrelevance of the Big Bang itself, but instead the irrelevance of "any events before the Big Bang" (Hawking 2002, 105). For our purposes at this point, that change makes little difference.

8. For the origins of my use of the term *imaginative construction*, see the epilogue, section III.

9. The subtitle of Deacon's book is "The Co-evolution of Language and the Brain." Symbols, as he argues (partially drawing on Charles Sanders Peirce), are not simple iconic signs, in which a noise or mark stands for some object in the world (a so-called indexical reference [Deacon 1997, 70ff.]), although "symbolic reference depends upon indexical reference" (74). Words, for instance, often (though not always) represent objects in the world, but they also "represent other words. In fact, they are incorporated into quite specific individual relationships to *all* other words in a language. . . . It is by virtue of this sort

of dual reference, to objects and to other words (or at least to other semantic alternatives) that a word conveys the information necessary to pick out objects of reference. . . . This referential relationship between the words—words systematically indicating other words—forms a system of higher order relationships. . . . Symbolic reference derives from *combinatorial* possibilities and impossibilities. . . . What determines the pairing between a symbol (like a word) and some object or event is not their probability of co-occurrence, but rather some complex function of the relationship that the symbol has to other symbols" (82-83). "In summary, then, symbols cannot be understood as an unstructured collection of tokens. . . . Because of this systematic relational basis of symbolic reference, no collection of signs can function symbolically unless the entire collection conforms to certain overall principles of organization. . . . The structure implicit in the symbol-symbol mapping is not present before symbolic reference, but comes into being and affects symbol combinations from the moment it is first constructed. . . . The system of representational relationships, which develops between symbols as symbol systems grow, comprises an ever more complex matrix. . . . Because symbolic reference is inherently systemic, there can be no symbolization without systematic relationships" (99-100).

10. We must never forget that "Although the movements of history are shaped in many ways by human decisions and actions, much more is going on in them than simply the realization of deliberate human intentions. Columbus was looking for an easier way to India, but what he did was 'discover' America. A group of Dutch settlers founded New Amsterdam in 1623, but in their wildest dreams they could not have foreseen the modern New York City that was to grow out of their colony. The Magna Charta was signed in 1215 by King John to guarantee certain feudal rights to some nobles, but in due course it became a significant foundation for the development of English constitutional liberties and modern Anglo-Saxon democracy. The invention of moveable type by Johannes Gutenberg made possible completely unanticipated developments in modern culture

through making the printed word available to almost everyone. And so on. Many events, which might seem rather small and insignificant when they occur, turn out to have far-reaching unforeseen consequences, sometimes transforming the course of history in quite unexpected ways . . . what I call 'the serendipity of history'" (Kaufman 1993a, 273–75).

11. Complexity theory is more sweepingly comprehensive than biological evolutionary theory in that it develops overarching concepts dealing with inorganic complexity as well as the complexity of life. The neo-Darwinian theory of evolution through chance variations and natural selection is taken up (with some alterations) into this more comprehensive account of the emergence of increasingly complex forms of order. For discussion of the relations of evolutionary theory to complexity theory, see Taylor 2001, 182–94.

12. For a sketch of the complexity of human selfhood and community that underlies human intentional action, moral responsibility, and creativity—and without which none of these would be possible—see Kaufman 1993a, chapters 11 to 13.

13. For discussion of this infinitude, see Steiner 1989, part II.

14. A fuller presentation and elaboration of humans as biohistorical beings can be found in Kaufman 1993a, part II.

15. As I mentioned above (footnote 7), Stephen Hawking has noted this extremely ambiguous situation, and has declared, "one might as well cut the big bang, and any events before it, out of the theory" (Hawking 1988, 122). The change in his later text, no longer applying this drastic remark to the Big Bang itself but only to "any events before the big bang" (Hawking 2002, 105), is very interesting; but it does more, I think, to conceal from us the mystery here than to illuminate it.

16. This remark (and others in this chapter) suggests that the three-modality framework for thinking about creativity sketched here implies that creativity$_1$ is the basic template in terms of which the meaning of the word "creativity" is defined and elaborated. With the model of *creatio ex nihilo* in mind, creativities$_{2,3}$ inevitably appear to be deficient forms (in certain respects), though they clearly manifest

characteristics that are analogous to the defining form. Linguistic and historical arguments could be provided to justify giving conceptual priority to creativity$_1$, but they would not be conclusive. It would also be possible to present an analysis of creativity in which creativity$_2$ was taken as the defining paradigm. (The paradigm for the biblical writers was creativity$_3$, but in today's world that is not plausible, as we have seen.) This would lead to a significantly different picture, one in which creativity$_1$ would likely appear to be an abstraction with important contextual features of that creativity simply unknown. I cannot pursue these matters here. I mention them because I think they would be well worth exploring further as we seek to understand better the degree to which and the respects in which the concept of creativity can be regarded as appropriate for constructive work in theology today.

17. Nearly a century ago, A. N. Whitehead saw clearly the necessity and propriety of such a claim. See his "bipolar" conception of God in *Process and Reality* (1929, 521–33).

18. I do not wish to push this point, but it is interesting to note that there is some resemblance (though by no means an identity) between the three-fold structure of creativity that has been outlined here and the Christian notion of God as Trinity: creativity$_1$ corresponds to the "first person"; creativity$_2$ to the "third person" (God's spirit active everywhere); and creativity$_3$ to the "second person" (God's incarnation in human existence and activity). The conception of God as creativity sometimes seems to connect with traditional Christian thinking in surprising ways.

19. For some speculations and references along this line, see epilogue, n. 13.

20. See especially (among many other passages) Mark 12:28-34; 1 Cor. 13; 1 John 4:7-21.

21. For consideration of the respects in which this line of thought may provide a theological basis for Christian pacifism today, see my article "Is God Nonviolent?" (Kaufman 2003). See also chapter 2 of this book.

22. God's "sustaining" activity is to be understood in terms of the cumulative structuring and ordering consequences of creativity in all three modalities.

23. What would it mean to be committed to and to worship a God such as this? (See Kaufman 1993a, especially chapters 24, 26, and 29; see also chapter 2 of this book.) A concluding remark on certain ethical implications of this theology of creativity should be made. My teacher, H. Richard Niebuhr, argued that we humans should always seek to live and act in response to what God is doing in the world and in our lives:"To discern the ways of God not in supernatural but in all natural and historic events, to respond to his intention present in and beyond and through all finite intentions, that is the way of responsibility to God. It is a way of universal responsibility because there is no action in the whole extent of actuality in which the universal intention, the meaning of the One beyond the many, is not present" (Niebuhr 1963, 170). The pertinence of this notion to the basic theme of this book is obvious: we should always seek to respond to the creativity manifest in the situation in which we find ourselves, creativity in the natural order as well as in the historical orders within which we are living. How does one discern what is truly "creative" in this complex world of events and actions? This will always be, of course, a judgment call in which we could well be mistaken. (That is also the case with Niebuhr's formulation.) However, if we take seriously into account our growing ecological knowledge, on the one hand, and the guidance provided by the New Testament christic images and teachings, on the other, we can begin to frame ways to address this problem: whatever appears to be moving toward a more sustainable ecological order on planet Earth and toward a more humane and loving civilization and society should be responded to affirmatively and supported in our own intentions and actions. Thus our activities and projects, we can hope, will become blended into the creativity at work in producing such a world. We should, of course, seek this creativity not only in programs and projects to which we ourselves are committed, but also in activities and events about which

we are inclined to be very critical or even to despise. For it may be precisely as we open ourselves to the serendipitous creativity at work in events and movements alien to our inclinations that we will come to deeper insight and understanding of the creativity actually at work in our world and thus be enabled to respond creatively to that creativity.

Epilogue

1. Quoted in Malcolm 1994, 1. What I mean by this remark, in applying it to myself, is probably quite different from what Wittgenstein meant by it (though there may also be some significant similarities). I hope my meaning will come clear in the course of this epilogue.

2. For a general statement about the background of my theological work, see "Some Reflections on a Theological Pilgrimage" (Kaufman 1994); for those who want to know more about how my Mennonite background has influenced my thinking, see Kaufman 1988 and the article entitled "The Mennonite Roots of My Theological Perspective" (Kaufman 1996b). Short pieces on specific themes in my work include "The Influence of Feminist Theory on my Theological Work" (Kaufman 1991).

3. In two early articles (among others), I explored some aspects of this central Mennonite conviction: "Some Theological Emphases of the Early Swiss Anabaptists" (Kaufman 1951) and "Nonresistance and Responsibility" (Kaufman 1958). See also *The Context of Decision* (Kaufman 1961). Some more recent articles bearing on this theme: "Jesus as Absolute Norm? Some Questions" (Kaufman 1993b), "The Mennonite Roots of My Theological Perspective" (Kaufman 1996b), and "Mennonite Peace Theology in a Religiously Plural World" (Kaufman 1996c).

4. A more explicit and detailed analysis of this matter can be found in Kaufman 1995, chapters 2 and 3.

5. I found H. Richard Niebuhr's book, *The Meaning of Revelation* (1941) particularly helpful.

6. A brief sketch of this way of thinking about religious truth-claims can be found in my last book, *God–Mystery–Diversity: Christian*

Theology in a Pluralistic World (Kaufman 1996a), chapters 12 and 13. The earliest steps in this direction are to be found in my 1958 essay on "Nonresistance and Responsibility" (Kaufman 1958).

7. The phrase, "imaginative construction," was probably derived from my dissertation on R. G. Collingwood, who used it to characterize the historian's act of putting together into a coherent account the historical materials with which he or she was working; see especially *The Idea of History* (Collingwood 1946, 241–49). I used the term frequently in my PhD dissertation and in my first book based on the dissertation (Kaufman 1960); see, for example, pp. 44f., 93, 102.

8. This book and its title were inspired in part by R. G. Collingwood's *An Essay on Philosophical Method* (1933).

9. Modifications in this stance, necessitated by the constructive theology I eventually published (Kaufman 1993a) are discussed in the third edition of *An Essay on Theological Method* (1995).

10. Many of these essays have been collected and published in books (Kaufman 1979, 1981, and 1985). This last book has been translated into German, Italian, Japanese, and Korean.

11. First published in Kaufman 1972b, 337–62, and later reprinted (with some alterations) as chapter 8 of Kaufman 1981.

12. First published in the *Journal of the American Academy of Religion* (Kaufman 1983) and later, with some revisions, becoming the first chapter of my book *Theology for a Nuclear Age* (Kaufman 1985). The quotation in the text is from the version in this book.

13. A couple of years after this I presented a paper entitled "God and Emptiness" to the Buddhist-Christian dialogue group of which I was a member. In this "experimental" piece I explored respects in which our understanding of God would be revolutionized if we dropped our (almost universal) presupposition—taken over from Greek metaphysical reflection—that God must be thought of in terms of the concept of *being* (either as "a being" or as "being itself"), substituting instead the Buddhist notion of *emptiness* (*sunyata*) as our most fundamental metaphysical concept. Such a change would lead to radical reconception of what we mean by God. It would thoroughly

undermine our Western thinking of God in reified notions of power (omnipotence), and would open theologians to much more radically christomorphic ideas of God's "weakness" and "nonresistance"—a Mennonite-grounded proposal that I had earlier made in Kaufman 1968 (see pp. 219ff., and 493ff.). These sorts of reflection, I think, helped prepare me to give up the substantival thinking of most traditional conceptions of God as I worked out the notion of God as "serendipitous creativity." This paper was first published as Kaufman 1989b. It has been republished (with some additions) in Kaufman 1996a (pp. 141–56).

14. A briefer presentation of the basic theological position worked out in *In Face of Mystery*, together with specific discussion of the bearing of that position on the problems posed for theology by human religious and cultural diversity, was published three years later in Kaufman 1996a.

Aquinas, Thomas. [1271] 1964. *Summa Theologiae*. New York: McGraw-Hill.

Augustine, Saint, Bishop of Hippo. [388-95] 1993. *On Free Choice of the Will*. Trans. Thomas Williams. Indianapolis: Hackett.

———. [400-16] 1963. *The Trinity*. Trans. Stephen McKenna. Vol. 45 of *Fathers of the Church*. Washington, D.C.: Catholic Univ. of America Press.

Barrow, John D., and Frank J. Tipler. 1988. *The Anthropic Cosmological Principle*. Oxford: Oxford Univ. Press.

Barth, Karl. [1918] 1933. *The Epistle to the Romans*. Trans. E. C. Hoskyns. London: Oxford Univ. Press.

Bellah, Robert. 1970. *Beyond Belief*. New York: Harper and Row.

Berdyaev, Nicholas J. 1937. *The Destiny of Man*. London: Geoffrey Bles.

Broad, William J. 2000. Maybe We Are Alone in the Universe, After All. *New York Times*, February 8.

Christ, Carol. 1997. *Rebirth of the Goddess: Finding Meaning in Feminist Spirituality*. Reading, Mass.: Addison-Wesley.

Collingwood, R. G. 1933. *An Essay on Philosophical Method*. Oxford: Clarendon.

———. 1946. *The Idea of History*. London: Oxford Univ. Press.

Daly, Mary. 1973. *Beyond God the Father: Toward a Philosophy of Women's Liberation*. Boston: Beacon.

Deacon, Terrence. 1997. *The Symbolic Species: The Co-evolution of Language and the Brain*. New York: Norton.

Denison, D. C. 2002. Playing with Billions. *Boston Globe Magazine*, December 29: 20–23, 29–31.

Diamond, Jared. 1997. *Guns, Germs, and Steel: The Fates of Human Societies*. New York: Norton.

Eckhart, Meister. [c. 1300] 1941. *Meister Eckhart: A Modern Translation*. Ed. and trans. Raymond B. Blakney. New York: Harper.

Feuerbach, Ludwig. [1841] 1957. *The Essence of Christianity*. Trans. George Eliot. New York: Harper & Bros.

Fiorenza, Francis Schüssler. 1984. *Foundational Theology*. New York: Crossroad.

Fiorenza, Francis Schüssler, and Gordon D. Kaufman. (See Kaufman and Fiorenza 1998)

Geertz, Clifford. 1973. *The Interpretation of Cultures*. New York: Basic Books.

Hawking, Stephen W. 1988. *A Brief History of Time: From the Big Bang to Black Holes*. New York: Bantam Books.

———. 2002. *The Theory of Everything: The Origin and Fate of the Universe*. Beverly Hills, Calif.: New Millenium.

James, William. [1902] 1985. *The Varieties of Religious Experience*. Cambridge: Harvard Univ. Press.

———. [1909] 1977. *A Pluralistic Universe*. Cambridge: Harvard Univ. Press.

———. 1920. *The Letters of William James*. Vol. 2. Ed. Henry James. Boston: Atlantic Monthly Press.

John of Damascus. [c. 743] 1899. *Exposition of the Orthodox Faith*. In *Select Works of Hilary of Poitiers and John of Damascus*. Vol. 9 of

A Select Library of Nicene and Post-Nicene Fathers of the Christian Church. Second Series. Oxford: Parker.

Kant, Immanuel. [1781] 1929. *Critique of Pure Reason.* Trans. Norman Kemp Smith. New York: St. Martin's.

Kaufman, Gordon D. 1951. Some Theological Emphases of the Early Swiss Anabaptists. *Mennonite Quarterly Review* 25 (2): 75–99.

———. 1955. The Problem of Relativism and the Possibility of Metaphysics: A Constructive Development of Certain Ideas in R. G. Collingwood, Wilhelm Dilthey, and Paul Tillich. PhD diss., Yale Univ.

———. 1958. Nonresistance and Responsibility. In *Concern: A Pamphlet Series for Questions of Christian Renewal,* no. 6: 5–29.

———. 1960. *Relativism, Knowledge, and Faith.* Chicago: Univ. of Chicago Press.

———. 1961. *The Context of Decision.* New York: Abingdon.

———. 1968. *Systematic Theology: A Historicist Perspective.* New York: Scribner.

———. 1972a. *God the Problem.* Cambridge: Harvard Univ. Press.

———. 1972b. A Problem for Theology: The Concept of Nature. *Harvard Theological Review* 65 (3): 337–66.

———. 1979. *Nonresistance and Responsibility, and Other Mennonite Essays.* Newton, Kans.: Faith and Life.

———. 1981. *The Theological Imagination: Constructing the Concept of God.* Philadelphia: Westminster.

———. 1983. Nuclear Eschatology and the Study of Religion. *Journal of the American Academy of Religion* 51 (1): 3-14.

———. 1985. *Theology for a Nuclear Age.* Manchester, UK: Univ. of Manchester Press; Philadelphia: Westminster.

———. 1988. Apologia Pro Vita Sua. In *Why I Am a Mennonite: Essays on Mennonite Identity,* ed. Harry Loewen, 126–38. Scottdale, Pa.: Herald.

———. 1989a. Evidentialism: A Theologian's Response. *Faith and Philosophy* 6 (1): 35–46.

————. 1989b. God and Emptiness: An Experimental Essay. *Buddhist-Christian Studies* 9: 175–87. Also published (in a slightly different version) in *The Religious Philosophy of Nishitani Keiji*, ed. Taitetso Unno, 82–97. Berkeley: Asian Humanities; and (with some additions) in Kaufman 1996a.

————. 1991. The Influence of Feminist Theory on My Theological Work. *Journal of Feminist Studies in Religion* 7 (1): 112–15.

————. 1993a. *In Face of Mystery: A Constructive Theology.* Cambridge: Harvard Univ. Press.

————. 1993b. Jesus as Absolute Norm? Some Questions. In *The Limits of Perfection: A Conversation with J. Lawrence Burkholder*, ed. R.J. Sawatsky and Scott Holland, 118–21. Waterloo, ON: Institute of Anabaptist-Mennonite Studies.

————. 1994. Some Reflections on a Theological Pilgrimage. *Religious Studies Review* 20 (3): 177–81.

————. 1995. *An Essay on Theological Method.* 3rd ed. New York: Oxford Univ. Press. First edition 1975 by Scholars.

————. 1996a. *God—Mystery—Diversity: Christian Theology in a Pluralistic World.* Minneapolis: Fortress Press.

————. 1996b. The Mennonite Roots of My Theological Perspective. In *Mennonite Theology in Face of Modernity: Essays in Honor of Gordon D. Kaufman*, ed. Alain Epp Weaver, 1-19. Newton, Kans.: Bethel College.

————. 1996c. Mennonite Peace Theology in a Religiously Plural World. *Conrad Grebel Review* 14 (1): 33-47.

————. 2000. Ecological Consciousness and the Symbol 'God.' In *Christianity in the 21st Century*, ed. Deborah A. Brown, 72-95. New York: Crossroad.

————. 2001a. On Thinking of God as Serendipitous Creativity. *Journal of the American Academy of Religion* 69 (2): 409–25.

————. 2001b. My Life and My Theological Reflection: Two Themes. *American Journal of Theology and Philosophy* 22 (1): 3–32.

———. 2003. Is God Nonviolent? *Conrad Grebel Review* 21 (1): 18–24.

Kaufman, Gordon D., and Francis Schüssler Fiorenza. 1998. God. In *Critical Terms for Religious Studies*, ed. Mark C. Taylor. Chicago: Univ. of Chicago Press.

Lévinas, Emmanuel. 1969. *Totality and Infinity*. Pittsburgh: Duquesne Univ. Press.

Maimonides, Moses. [1190] 1963. *The Guide of the Perplexed*. Trans. and ed. Shlomo Pines. Chicago: Univ. of Chicago Press.

Malcolm, Norman. 1994. *Wittgenstein: A Religious Point of View?* Ithaca: Cornell Univ. Press.

Marion, Jean-Luc. 1991. *God without Being*. Chicago: Univ. of Chicago Press.

Mathews, Shailer. 1924. *The Faith of Modernism*. New York: Macmillan.

———. 1931. *The Growth of the Idea of God*. New York: Macmillan.

McFague, Sallie. 1987. *Models of God: Theology for an Ecological Nuclear Age*. Philadelphia: Fortress Press.

Mead, George Herbert. 1934. *Mind, Self, and Society*. Chicago: Univ. of Chicago Press.

Nicholas of Cusa. [1440] 1954. *Of Learned Ignorance*. New Haven: Yale Univ. Press.

Niebuhr, H. Richard. 1941. *The Meaning of Revelation*. New York: Macmillan.

———. 1960. *Radical Monotheism and Western Culture*. New York: Harper.

———. 1963. *The Responsible Self*. New York: Harper and Row.

Otto, Rudolf. [1917] 1950. *The Idea of the Holy*. 2nd ed. London: Oxford Univ. Press.

Overbye, Dennis. 2002. In the Beginning... *New York Times*, July 23.

Oxford English Dictionary. 1971. Compact ed. New York: Oxford Univ. Press.

Pascal, Blaise. [c. 1670] 1995. *Pensées and Other Writings*. Trans. Homer Levi. New York: Oxford Univ. Press.

Plato. [366-360] 1937. *The Timaeus*. In *Plato's Cosmology*, trans. F. M. Cornford. London: Routledge & Kegan Paul.

Polkinghorne, John. 1996. Chaos Theory and Divine Action. In *Religion and Science: History, Method, Dialogue*, ed. W. Mark Richardson and Wesley J. Wildman, 243–52. New York: Routledge.

Pseudo-Dionysius. [sixth century] 1951. *On the Divine Names, and Mystical Theology*. Trans. C. E. Rolt. London: Society for Promoting Christian Knowledge.

Rees, Martin. 1997. *Before the Beginning: Our Universe and Others*. Reading, Mass.: Addison-Wesley.

Rue, Loyal. 2000. *Everybody's Story*. Albany: SUNY Press.

Ruether, Rosemary Radford. 1992. *Gaia and God: An Ecofeminist Theology of Earth Healing*. San Francisco: Harper.

Schleiermacher, Friedrich. [1799] 1958. *On Religion: Speeches to Its Cultured Despisers*. New York: Harper.

———. [1811] 1976. *Dialektik*, ed. Rudolf Odebrecht. Darmstadt: Wissenschaftliche Buchgesellschaft.

———. [1822] 1928. *The Christian Faith*. Trans. H. R. Mackintosh and J. S. Stewart. Edinburgh: Clark.

Schüssler Fiorenza, Elisabeth. 1993. *In Memory of Her*. New York: Crossroad.

Spinoza, Baruch. [1677] 1989. *Ethics*. Trans. Andrew Boyle, revised by H. R. Parkinson. London: Dent.

Steiner, George. 1989. *Real Presences*. Chicago: Univ. of Chicago Press.

Taylor, Mark C. 2001. *The Moment of Complexity: Emerging Network Culture*. Chicago: Univ. of Chicago Press.

Theissen, Gerd. 1985. *Biblical Faith: An Evolutionary Approach*. Philadelphia: Fortress Press.

Whitehead, Alfred North. 1929. *Process and Reality*. New York: Macmillan.

Wieman, Henry Nelson. 1946. *The Source of Human Good*. Chicago: Univ. of Chicago Press.

Made in the USA
San Bernardino, CA
21 June 2014